Endorsements
8 Ways to Sustainable Wellbeing
For Teens and Their Families

People are saying …

"A must-have resource for all therapists and for anyone working with adolescents and young adults. In a down-to-earth tone and with practical recommendations, this book guides teens on the journey of self-help and development. A focus on wellbeing has increasingly become of interest to educators, behavioral health providers and pediatricians seeking a holistic approach to helping healthy and struggling adolescent become more self-actualized. These exercises can be done with the entire family, as an opportunity to help everyone focus on growth and optimism."

—Guy Diamond, Ph.D., Professor Emeritus, University of Pennsylvania School of Medicine; Director, Center for Family Intervention Science, Drexel University; developer of Attachment-Based Family Therapy

"As an addictions and mental health counselor with over two decades of professional experience, I find that this book brings a comprehensive and integrative lens to the field, which is so needed today. I highly recommend this workbook to any family who is interested in doing this beneficial work."

—Wendy Adamson, C.A.D.C. II, author of *Mother Load: A Memoir of Addiction, Gun Violence & Finding a Life of Purpose*

"Navigating the teen years is possibly the biggest challenge to one's mental wellness. Too often, teens turn to substance abuse, social media, self-harm and video games as a way to cope with their symptoms of depression, despair, anxiety, and hopelessness. The easy-to-follow format of this timely and much-needed workbook will provide help for teens, parents and therapists. Those who read this book and integrate its teachings, accompanied by psychotherapy, will find it extremely helpful in making changes to maladaptive patterns of mental and physical health—changes that will last a lifetime."

—Scott Barshack, M.D., Medical Director, Paradigm Teen Treatment Center

"Awareness and self-love are paramount for spiritual, physical and emotional wellness. *8 Ways to Sustainable Wellbeing: For Teens and Their Families* offers practical and relatable tips, tools and exercises to engage and inspire teens to be mindful participants in their recovery and to experience life-long change."
  —Dr. Denise McDermott, Integrative Psychiatrist

"A brilliant tool for reaching young people—as well as their families—and helping them to embrace the essence of holistic recovery, this workbook guides readers through the process of incorporating therapeutic lifestyle changes that lead to a truly balanced approach to personal growth and wellness."
  —Jim Savage, L.C.D.C., Dallas Recovery Center

"What an exceptional and timely workbook for the adolescent and family in recovery. Dr. Weedn and Jamison Monroe lead them through a process filled with learning and uncovering awareness, and invite readers to develop a complete, thorough and fully explored plan for success. The engaging practices and activities specific to adolescent development will capture teens' interest and keep them committed to the process of self-evolving and discovery. This workbook will be a welcome friend to teens and families, and a valuable tool for therapists."
  —Paulette Tomasson, R.N., Registered Clinical Counsellor

"Change begins with awareness and is realized through action. *8 Ways to Sustainable Wellbeing* is a masterfully curated plan to accomplish both."
  —Peter Fluor, C.E.O. and founder, Driftwood Recovery

"Straightforward and to the point, this foundational workbook outlines what is essentially a receipt for a happy life—and there is no better time to begin these practices than in the teenage years, when you are building the person you will become. It's easy to read, covers the areas that really matter and provides exercises to personalize your journey towards a state of wellness, vitality, purpose and meaning."
  —Tian Dayton, Ph.D., author of *Emotional Sobriety, The Soulful Journey of Recovery*

8 Ways to Sustainable Wellbeing
For Teens and Their Families

8 Ways to Sustainable Wellbeing
For Teens and Their Families

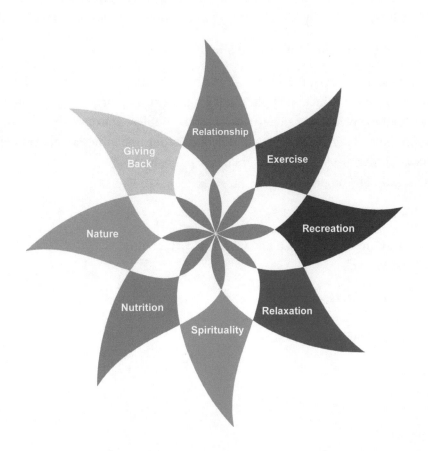

By Sonnee D. Weedn, Ph.D., and Jamison Monroe

ISBN Paperback: 978-0-9832776-3-7

Interior Book Design: Ghislain Viau and Chelsea Cartabiano
Cover Art: Lisa Wenrick

Printed in the United States of America
Publisher: Chispa Publishing, Novato, CA
https://www.ChispaPublishing.com

8 Ways to Sustainable Wellbeing
For Teens and Their Families

Mission Statement: To inform, inspire, support and empower all teens to optimize their mental health through therapeutic lifestyle changes, with the support of their family. This workbook is intended to educate the reader on an integrated approach to creating and sustaining behavior-change strategies for increased health, wellness and resilience throughout their lifetime.

Acknowledgments

The framework that informs *8 Ways to Sustainable Wellbeing For Teens and Their Families* was developed by Roger Walsh, M.D., Ph.D. We thank him for his original research and for so graciously supporting the development of this workbook.

Special thanks to Lisa Wenrick, who created the graphic design featured on the cover of this book and others in the series. Her sensitivity to the content resulted in an elegant logo that artistically conveys the heart of our work. Also to Suanna Van Norstrand, Chelsea Cartabiano and Tresca Weinstein for their commitment to seeing this project to fruition.

Deep gratitude also goes to Lorien Fenton for her eye to detail and her eternal optimism in moving this project forward.

We are grateful for our many teachers and guides, as well as for the families who come to us in need of assistance, and who trust themselves and their children to our guidance.

Table of Contents

Foreword

My trusted friends and professional colleagues, Sonnee Weedn and Jamison Monroe, have combined their experience and wisdom to provide essential guidance for young people and their families who are seeking health and recovery. I could not be more pleased to recommend this timely work.

Dr. Weedn's first workbook, *8 Ways to Wellbeing for Recovering People*, is a codification of the research of Roger Walsh, M.D., Ph.D., at the University of California at Irvine, on optimizing mental health. Though written for the recovering community, the information is completely relevant for us all.

Now she has adapted *8 Ways* specifically for teens and families in collaboration with Jamison Monroe, founder of Newport Academy, a teen treatment program with locations around the United States. Newport Academy and its sister program, Newport Institute for young adults, offer family-focused and results-oriented programs addressing the underlying causes and conditions of destructive behaviors. "We provide the highest-quality care to bring sustainable healing to teens and young adults who are struggling as I once was," says Jamison.

Navigating the teen years is possibly the biggest challenge to mental wellness, which can be compromised by trauma, lack of support and unhelpful lifestyles and patterns of thinking. Too often, teens turn to substance abuse, social media, self-harm and video games as ways to cope with their symptoms of depression, loneliness, despair, anxiety and hopelessness.

Wellbeing, on the other hand, is the experience of health, happiness and prosperity. It includes having good mental health, high life satisfaction, a sense of meaning or purpose and the ability to manage stress. More generally, wellbeing is just feeling well. A focus on wellbeing has increasingly become of interest to educators, behavioral health providers and pediatricians seeking an integrative approach to helping healthy and struggling adolescents become more self-actualized.

In a straightforward fashion, *8 Ways to Sustainable Wellbeing For Teens and Their Families* offers practical and relatable tips, tools and exercises to engage and inspire teens to become mindful participants in their recovery and to experience lifelong change. It leads young people and their families through a process filled with learning and uncovering awareness, and invites readers to develop a complete, thorough and fully explored plan for success.

I wish you well on your journey of discovery.

Gary Seidler
Co-Founder, Health Communications
US Journal of Drug & Alcohol Dependence
US Journal Training

Preface

Recovery from Anything

Recovery from mental health challenges of any kind, including co-occurring disorders such as substance abuse, eating disorders, self-harm, gaming, depression, anxiety and so forth, is complicated, because it touches most every aspect of a person's life. Almost always, professional help is indicated to break free. What are frequently overlooked in many behavioral health treatment settings are the very real changes in mental as well as physical health that can take place when particular attention is paid to therapeutic lifestyle changes, which we will refer to as TLCs.

Optimizing Your Mental Health

This workbook is designed to optimize teenagers' mental health and addiction recovery work and create a program to enhance their general health and wellbeing. A decision about making this a way of life is a decision to improve your physical and mental health, in general. We hope that it is just the beginning of learning about the various aspects of wellness that provide the best opportunities to live well in the long run. This program is supported and informed by the research of Dr. Roger Walsh, M.D., at the University of California at Irvine. This integrated approach to teen mental health treatment is practiced at Newport Academy, Newport Healthcare's nationally recognized healing centers for ages 12–17.

To optimize mental health or begin a recovery program, be it from chemical dependency or other co-occurring disorders, good intentions and will alone are not enough to assure success.

Successful Long-Term Recovery

Successful, long-term recovery takes a realistic, personalized, informed plan; the intention and will to follow the plan meticulously; and an experienced person or community who supports your recovery. Accountability to another person or a group will prove helpful in this endeavor. We believe that our greatest healing takes place in community. So, we hope teens will consider embarking on this program with a friend or a group who can help them set reasonable goals and be accountable to them. As they say, "Progress, not Perfection."

This workbook contains all of the ingredients to create that realistic, personalized and informed plan to be used in addition to a residential or outpatient treatment program, possible 12-Step membership, and continuing therapy. When used in conjunction with a support group of some sort or a therapist, it is an extremely powerful tool.

Identifying Your Support Group

Because we have suggested using this workbook in conjunction with a therapist, a group or a friend, we hope teens will begin by identifying that support, searching for the right person or group to assist them. Then, in conjunction with that person or group, they can formulate a plan and write the name/names of their support person(s) in the space below. If environments or situations change, please update this area as needed.

To Recovering Teens

Congratulations! You are about to embark on a fabulous healing journey.

People Who Support Me Getting Healthy

Name	Telephone	Email	Relationship

Introduction: Let's Get Started

Begin Well

It is important to begin well, and setting clear intention is a good way to start. Please sit back in your seat for a moment and reflect on what you hope to have achieved in your recovery by the time one year has passed. Think about what you hope your life is like. Close your eyes for just a minute now and get an image of yourself healthy in every possible way. Good! Now that you have that picture in your mind's eye, write a brief paragraph of what you wish for yourself one year from now. Be very, very specific and make sure that whatever you are intending is measurable.

_____

_____

_____

_____

_____

_____

_____

_____

_____

Now that you have an idea or an image in mind, write a few goals that will help you achieve that image and the reasonable length of time you believe it will take you to achieve those goals.

Personal Goal	Time to Achieve Goal
1)	
2)	
3)	
4)	
5)	

Now write down what the main benefits will be to you as you pursue these goals. Refer specifically to each one that you have written.

Personal Goal	Benefits of Pursuing Goal
1)	
2)	
3)	
4)	
5)	

Great! Now write a bit about how you might sabotage these goals (we all have that saboteur in us, you know). When we know ourselves well, we know some of the ways in which we might get off track.

Now write some ideas about what you will do to get yourself back on track when and if the Saboteur has taken over. Be specific.

What Sabotages Personal Goal	How to Get Back On Track
1)	
2)	
3)	
4)	
5)	

Most people enjoy being rewarded in some way when they can eliminate detrimental habits and behaviors, and replace them with health-promoting ones. What would be some healthy ways that you can reward yourself when you are on track with your goals? List at least five possibilities.

1. _____

2. _____

3. _____

4. _____

5. _____

Great! This section where you set intention and examined your process a bit is now complete. Before continuing, use the space below to draw a picture symbolizing your mental well-being. This can be realistic or symbolic ... you choose. Use crayons or colored pencils to really make your picture come to life!

Directions for Using This Workbook

This book can be used by both teens and their parents, and families are encouraged to read it together. For younger teens, reading this book and doing the exercises included here may be more productive with a parent or other trusted adult alongside. In fact, doing so may serve as a bonding experience for you. Older teens might find all of this book useful, or may resonate with particular ideas at this time, and then return to the book later and discover more richness in the guidance found here once they are in a new stage of their recovery.

First, it's essential to understand that substance use, eating disorders, self-harm, gaming addictions and other so-called co-occurring disorders or process addictions are generally a response to stress or trauma in the absence of healthier coping strategies. Either way, the brain and body will require time and attention to recover. Beyond the initial achievement of seeking treatment and, in the case of substance abuse, finding sobriety, which is no small thing, it will be important for teens to achieve and maintain a sense of wellbeing to guard against relapse. That's the point of this workbook. It is not a fundamental program of recovery, but an adjunct program to help teens create an overall sense of wellbeing through therapeutic lifestyle changes, which we will refer to as TLCs.

This is not meant to take the place of psychotherapy or properly supervised medication, if that is necessary. But, these TLCs are a proven way to reduce some of the psychological symptoms and suffering that underlie mental health issues and addiction, such as feelings of anxiety and depression, agitation, anger, and trouble concentrating, as well as physical symptoms such as low energy and poor self-esteem. Often, these TLCs reduce or eliminate the need for psychiatric medication and head off future problems.

Teens using this workbook are either just starting the healing process or have decided to enhance their treatment program by learning about and doing more to attain and maintain mental health and wellbeing. That's great! Since the importance of lifestyle for mental health is little appreciated in our culture, and only a small minority of mental health professionals emphasize TLCs, we are excited to share this information.

So, let's take a look at the **8 Ways to Wellbeing**, and what science and research tell us about living wisely and well, with recovering people in mind!

1. **Nutrition:** You Are What You Eat
2. **Exercise:** We Are Designed to Move
3. **Relaxation:** Take a Deep Breath In, and Then… Just Let It Go
4. **Recreation:** Fun Is Fun-Damental
5. **Relationships:** We Influence Each Other and We Need Each Other
6. **Nature:** Time in Nature Is a Source Of Healing
7. **Giving Back:** Giving the Gift of Generosity
8. **Spirituality:** We Find Our Spiritual Path

Lifestyle Survey

Teens should start by assessing themselves in each of the *8 Ways to Wellbeing* that have been identified. Fill out the following questionnaire to determine your level of comfort and participation in each of the categories identified. When you have completed the questionnaire, you will have a better understanding of where you stand and what your areas of strength and challenge are. At that point, you can choose one or more areas that challenge you, read the introductory material on each, and make your action plan to introduce or enhance that area of recovery. This is also a good time to share this with your identified support person, family member, therapist or group.

~ 8 Ways to Sustainable Wellbeing For Teens and Their Families Lifestyle Survey ~

Lifestyle factors are critical to the physical and mental health of recovering teens (and everyone else, for that matter). For each of the Therapeutic Lifestyle Changes (TLCs) listed, please indicate your guestimate (on average) of how many hours or minutes per week you spend on each, and how many hours or minutes you would like to spend on each.

Name_____

Date of Birth _____ Today's Date _____

8 Ways to Sustainable Wellbeing	Actual Hours Per Week	Desired Hours Per Week
Nutrition (healthy choices)		
Exercise (sports, walking, yoga, gym, etc.)		
Giving Back (contributions, altruism)		
Relationships (family, friends, 12-Step meetings)		
Relaxation/Mindfulness (fight or flight vs. rest and digest)		
Recreation and Play (music, dance, games, movies, sober fun)		
Time in Nature (time spent outdoors)		
Spiritual Development (care of your soul)		

Other Obstacles to Optimal Health

It is often true that recovering teens have other health challenges that should be addressed at some point. Though it is not the purpose of this workbook to address these, make note of any other issues you identify that are obstacles to you obtaining optimal health. Just identify them and write a few notes to yourself about how and when you would like to address them. On the next page are a few possibilities, and you can add others that come to you.

Sleep Hygiene – Are you able to consistently get 7 to 8 hours of sleep a night? If not, this is problematic and should be addressed. Don't wait too long. Try to avoid all screen activity and bright lights one hour before bedtime. Set a regular bedtime and wake-up time and try to maintain it. This should help sleep problems you may encounter. Make some notes about your sleep habits. If you have been taking sleep aids of any kind, consult your doctor or healthcare professional about weaning off of them.

_____

_____

_____

_____

_____

_____

_____

Smoking, Vaping, Smokeless Tobacco – You don't need us to tell you that smoking, vaping, other forms of smoking (anything) and smokeless tobacco are all extremely detrimental to your health. What is your plan for cessation of all smoking, vaping and/or chewing? Make some notes about this and share with your support person(s). Yes, it is hard! But, it is vitally important and you will be so glad you did this. There are social aspects to smoking and vaping, but you can learn to socialize without hurting yourself! Be a leader, not a follower! Set the tone for your recovery!

_____

_____

_____

_____

_____

_____

Getting Started

You've taken the Inventory to assess your areas of strength among the 8 Ways, and your areas of challenge. Just because you found strengths doesn't mean you don't need to read the material we have provided for you. In fact, it might be wise to pick one of your areas of relative strength and read over the material to see how you might build on this strength and amplify it. Sometimes it's easier to get started on a project with something you have relative comfort with. In any case, all 8 Ways are presented in no particular order of importance. You can choose wherever you'd like to start. Read over the material and possibilities for implementing them. Then, create some goals to incorporate this therapeutic lifestyle change into your everyday life. Write them in the spaces provided and keep track using the daily tracker pages in the Appendix. Let's go!

MY GOALS FOR LIFESTYLE CHANGES

Nutrition: You Are What You Eat

Our food should be our medicine
and our medicine should be our food.
—Hippocrates

The Reasons Why

There is truth in the claim that you are what you eat. After all, the miracle of our bodies is that they use whatever food we provide for them and turn it into energy and the building blocks to renew our cells. The relationship you have with food has a large impact on your physical health, as well as your mental health. As we say at Newport Academy, the meal is medicine.

As we now know, we cannot separate mind and body. What affects the body affects the mind, and vice versa. What is obvious is that if you want to restore your body, with your brain being a vital part of that body, improving your diet and general nutrition is vitally important. Some might say that paying attention to our nutrition is a high form of self-care and self-love. But, most importantly, in this chapter, we are NOT talking about diet, as in "a diet." We are talking about diet and nutrition as a lifestyle commitment. There is a big difference, and we are hoping you will adopt these suggestions, which are general ones, as a lifestyle that is fundamental to recovery and general health. If you want further refinement to your own eating and nutrition, we advise consulting with a registered dietician or nutritionist to help customize your eating plans, based on your particular needs.

In this chapter, we will offer some general guidelines and information and help you take stock of where you are now and what might be possible for you to begin to improve this area of wellbeing.

Write a few sentences here about how you would evaluate your overall nutrition.

_____

_____

_____

_____

Do you eat fast food? _____ How often? _____

Do you eat fresh fruit? _____ What kind? _____

_____

How often? _____ Organic? _____

Do you eat fresh vegetables? _____ How often? _____

_____

What kind? _____ Organic? _____

Do you eat processed food (most anything that comes in a package or that does not resemble its original form)? _____

_____

_____

How often? _____ What kinds? _____

_____

_____

Do you eat red meat (beef, lamb, pork, etc.)? _____

How often? _____

Organically raised? _____ Factory farmed? _____

Do you know the difference between the two? _____

Do you eat fish or shellfish? _____ How often? _____

Do you check to make sure it was line caught as opposed to farmed?_____

Sustainably managed? _____

Do you drink diet or sugary sodas? _____ How often? _____

Do you drink "energy" drinks? _____How many and how often? _____

_____

_____

For parents reading this book, this chapter can serve as a guide for how to support your teen—and your entire family—to eat in a way that supports better mental and physical health. If you're a teen and you're living at home or at school, you may not be doing your own food shopping or have as much control over your nutritional choices as you will when you are an adult. However, the important thing to remember is that when we feel good about ourselves, we want to take good care of ourselves, including making healthy food choices. And that creates what's called a positive feedback loop, because when we eat better, we feel better, in both body and mind.

We are not suggesting that you have to be rigid about your diet and nutrition, but we do want you to begin thinking about the food you eat, how it is sourced and its impact on you, and to make informed choices wherever possible—whether that's in the grocery store, at your family's dinner table, or in the dining hall at school. Read labels on food that comes in a can or package of any kind, to consider if there are artificial coloring or chemicals in them and whether those things are good for your nutrition. If you eat animal protein, consider the means by which the animal was raised and slaughtered, because this will determine what that animal was made of before it became part of you. If it was factory raised, it is likely full of hormones, and antibiotics that are not good for you to consume. Also, factory-farmed animals are generally kept in inhumane conditions and are quite stressed and therefore full of cortisol (stress hormones) that are unhelpful to your general health and wellbeing.

Likewise, be aware that eating organic fruits, vegetables, and meat, as well as line-caught fish, means that you will have less exposure to toxins in pesticides, and antibiotics and hormones given to animals.

It is no secret that when the body, and therefore, the brain, have been exposed to toxic chemicals, they will begin to break down in ways that may not be noticeable at first or to the untrained eye. But when people with mental health conditions or addictions are given physicals that include evaluating vitamin and mineral deficiencies, as well as overall health of the body, they are often found to be less than optimally healthy and often deficient in important vitamins and minerals.

Also, in substance abuse cases, if the physical includes cognitive testing to determine the health of the brain, there will often prove to be cognitive slippage due to a combination of the toxic exposure of whatever chemicals (including alcohol) have been ingested, as well as generally poor nutrition. The good news is that the body and brain, given proper support, will usually be able to heal themselves and return to a state of health. Whatever support you can get through good nutrition will eventually lead to more physical strength, stamina and brain function.

Often, the images of a life in recovery are not very compelling. Recovery expert Tommy Rosen says, "The images of recovery we have been shown in books, television shows and movies depict very sick people who do not seem to be getting better. In fact, often when you go to 12-Step meetings, everyone is smoking, and drinking lots of coffee." He doesn't mention the intense craving for sugar that often comes in early recovery, but you can observe that, too.

Everyone has to start somewhere in recovery and just stopping the drinking and using is a great beginning. But, we are hoping for more than that! We are advocating for optimal health and wellbeing, to ensure ongoing recovery, and that takes time, effort and commitment.

Sadly, the advertising, factory farming, restaurant and packaged goods industries in Western society are geared toward encouraging unhealthy choices. Every day you are bombarded with ads encouraging you to consume sugar, alcohol, nicotine and fast food in the never-ending search for what the food industry calls the "bliss point" of "eatertainment" through "hyper-eating" enormous portions and empty calories. Unfortunately, you can never get enough of what you do NOT really need—but you can certainly ruin your health and lifestyle trying. Let's do better!

Irregular eating, fast food and generally poor diet tend to go hand in hand with mental health challenges and substance abuse. Teens with depression or anxiety often don't care enough about themselves to eat well. Chemically dependent people are typically more interested in their drug of choice than they are in the food they choose. Research shows connections between nutrition, behavior and recovery, and the important implications that must be addressed. For example, drug and/or alcohol addiction may cause a person to forget what it is like to be hungry and instead mistake this feeling for a drug craving. Read that sentence again! It was important!

In addition, many of the diseases associated with alcoholism are caused by nutritional deficiencies. This includes alcoholic liver disease and alcoholic dementia. The American Dietetic Association states that, "Nutrition intervention in treatment and recovery from chemical dependency is imperative. Many debilitating nutritional consequences result from drug and alcohol abuse. Chronic nutrition impairment causes serious damage to the liver and brain, which reinforces the craving for more drugs and alcohol and perpetuates the psychological aspect of the addiction. During treatment, efforts are concentrated on the physical recovery, providing adequate nutrition to replete and heal the brain, liver and digestive system. Nutrition makes a difference in the rate and quality of physical recovery, which prepares people to function at a higher level in treatment—cognitively, mentally, and socially. Improved nutritional status can make treatment more effective, while reducing drug and alcohol craving, thereby preventing relapse."

Once recovery is underway (including the completion of detox in substance abuse cases), it is vital to begin the process of rebuilding the brain and body through good nutrition. So, what follows is the general information to get you started. If you have an eating disorder or other nutritional concerns, be sure to consult your registered dietitian, nutritionist or healthcare provider.

For teens, eating out can be a fun and convenient opportunity for socializing—but it's also expensive and the food often contains high amounts of sodium (salt) and sugar. Knowing the actual ingredients of what is being served in a fast food outlet or other restaurant meal is almost impossible.

How often do you eat out rather than eating at home? _____

In the restaurants you frequent, are the calorie contents and ingredients in the dishes listed on the menu? _____

_____

What are your favorite places to eat out if you do? _____

_____

_____

_____

_____

Are they establishments that will support good nutrition and health? _____

_____

_____

_____

If they do support good nutrition, well, great. If not, any ideas about where else you might eat out that would be healthier and where you can actually discern what the ingredients are?

_____

_____

_____

Make nutrition and health a priority and choose wisely. Eat at places that support your goal of maintaining a health-enhancing lifestyle and avoid those that undermine your program. In addition, remember that restaurants will generally accommodate any requests you make, so ask for what you want.

So, what exactly is a healthy diet? There have been so many crazy diet schemes and fads in the media that it is hard to know what to do. Here are some very general guidelines, but please consult your physician, nutritionist or other medical advisor for more in-depth recommendations.

- Lots of fresh vegetables, organic if possible

- Healthy fats, such as olive oil

- Fresh fruit, organic if possible

- Meat, eggs and dairy, raised in as close to the animal's natural environment as possible (grass-fed cows, pasture-raised chickens, etc.)

- Limit processed foods. If it comes in a package, read the ingredients list carefully and avoid if there are ingredients whose names you don't recognize (often chemicals and dyes).

- No fast food

- Little or no sugar (or sugar substitutes), artificial sweeteners, preservatives or other ingredients you don't recognize or have trouble pronouncing

- Whole grains (no white flour)

Yes, it sounds challenging! And, it is! Remember that A.A. aphorism, *"Progress, not perfection."* Make some small changes and see how that goes, tackling one nutritional habit at a time. For example, make a goal of eating two or three fresh fruits each day. Track it for a while until it is a habit and see how it goes. When you are doing that consistently, choose another nutritional goal to add to the first one.

Possible Actions for Implementation

As much as possible, eat meals at home. Don't inhale your food standing up or on the go. Focus on the pleasures of eating. Cook with family or friends, eat together, talk together and make mealtime a relaxing experience. Eating together helps build close relationships.

Take charge of what you put in your body. Focus on what you need and the foods that will supply you with the nutrients required to optimize thinking and energy to do what you want to do.

Describe what you typically eat and drink in a day, including any supplements you take:

Morning	
Afternoon	
Evening	
Snacks	

An aspect of physical fitness is good nutrition, and physical fitness is defined as your mind and body's ability to function efficiently and effectively in activities, to be healthy, to resist disease, to have endurance and to recover normally. On a scale of 0 to 5, are you physically fit (5) or easily fatigued and unhealthy (0)?

Circle your level of fitness right now: 0   1   2   3   4   5

This chapter will help you know how to incorporate healthier eating habits into your life. These habits can further strengthen your body, improve brain function and help you overcome drug/alcohol cravings. The skills you learn and practice will help you keep your body as healthy and disease-free as possible to support recovery.

People in early recovery have often neglected to take care of the body. Being nutrition-savvy and eating a healthier diet will help your body recover. Sometimes feelings of fatigue, depression or anxiety are actually caused by early signs of malnutrition. Researchers exploring both neuro-circuitry and nutrition have found that eating well can not only help you feel better, but also promote clearer thinking and general brain health.

If you have food allergies or sensitivities, please list them here.

Write about your **attitude** toward making some changes to your diet and nutrition.

_____

_____

_____

_____

_____

_____

Being depressed, anxious or chemically dependent can change your appetite, and it may take a while to get your appetite back or get it in check once it does come back. If you are a recovering alcoholic, you may notice an intense craving for sugar. This is common. If you don't feel like eating, don't force yourself to eat a lot at one time. Have small meals that include foods that look good to you, and eat regularly to maintain your blood sugar levels and your energy.

Are you experiencing sugar cravings or other cravings that are unhelpful? What about cravings for soda? Understand that diet drinks are harmful to the brain and body and are to be avoided, so include those in your discussion.

_____

_____

_____

_____

_____

_____

_____

Do you overeat when stressed, bored, upset or tired? If you find that you're using food as a coping or control strategy, then try to problem solve using other strategies, such as relaxation, recreation, exercise or time in nature. Make small changes over a period of days, weeks and months so you'll stay with your program. Write below about any tendency to overeat or under-eat.

_____

_____

_____

_____

_____

_____

Eating in a healthy manner does not mean sacrificing taste and the pleasure that delicious food brings. However, food manufacturers use persuasive ads and alluring packaging to keep their processed foods tapping into your cravings. These foods contain chemical compounds that stimulate the brain's secretion of opiate-like, "feel-good" chemicals like dopamine, which drive cravings for sugary, salty or fatty foods. If your stomach is growling at the thought of potato chips, mocha latte grandé, cola and cookies, give yourself three weeks without them, and your tastes will change and you probably won't want the food as much. Parents, or teens who do food shopping, we advise you to select the freshest items available at the grocery store, fruit stand, fish market, specialty store, organic food cooperative—or grow your own. Farmer's markets are a wonderful place to shop for fresh fruits and vegetables, and sometimes meat raised and killed by the farmer you buy it from, and fish from the people who fished for it. Knowing where your food comes from is a powerful habit to adopt.

To keep your energy balanced all day, nutritionists typically advise three meals and two healthy snacks between meals each day. This will help keep you from feeling tired, and prevent mood swings and cravings. Eating well can enhance your ability to perform tasks and preserve cognitive functions, and may reduce symptoms of depression and anxiety.

Make a list here of healthy snacks that you can eat midmorning and midafternoon as part of your good nutrition program.

_____

_____

_____

_____

Overall, a rainbow diet of multicolored vegetables and fruits, grains and sources of protein, with various textures, is not only healthier, but also more enjoyable to look at and consume. So, before you take a bite of your food, look at the food arranged on your plate. Make sure there is a variety of colors represented and take a moment to appreciate the visual aspects of the food. Smell the food before you eat it as a means of further appreciation. Make a statement of gratitude before eating—gratitude for the farmers, suppliers and cooks, as well as for the food itself.

The body needs more than 50 different nutrients, like vitamins, each day. To get them, you need to eat a variety of foods. The main food groups are grains and legumes, vegetables and fruits, and dairy and meat products and alternatives. Please note that sugar and caffeine are NOT food groups!

A balanced diet needs to include all these different nutrients:

- **Complex Carbohydrates** are needed for energy
- **Protein** is needed so that the body can build and repair
- **Healthy Fats** also provide energy and they are required for some essential chemical reactions
- **Vitamins** are needed by the body in order to perform essential metabolic activities
- **Minerals** are necessary for metabolism and to keep the body functioning
- **Water** is essential as it accounts for 70% of the composition of the body. It provides a medium for chemical reactions.

If we fail to get enough of these nutrients, the body will suffer.

Alcohol use is one of the major causes of nutritional deficiency. Some vitamins important for mental health include iron, folate and vitamins B6 and B12. Deficiencies of any of these nutrients can mimic mental health problems such as depression, fatigue, poor attention and altered sleep. A lack of these nutrients causes anemia and nervous system problems. Damage to the liver and pancreas results in an imbalance of fluids, calories, protein and electrolytes. About 70 percent of people are Vitamin D deficient, and this rate is higher for substance abusers. Deficiencies may be implicated in cognitive impairment, depression and bipolar disorder. Ask your doctor or nutritionist about vitamin and mineral supplementation, if needed.

Protein is a major player in your diet. Because it has such an important function in the body, you need a fair share of protein every single day. The primary sources of protein are common meat products like chicken, beef, pork and fish. If you're trying to reduce your daily meat intake, try some of these sources of protein and additional vital nutrients: quinoa, soy products, Greek yogurt, cottage cheese, chia seeds, chickpeas (garbanzo beans), nuts, lentils, edamame, tofu, seitan, tempeh or peanut butter.

Dietary Fiber is also known as "roughage." It is the part of food that can't be broken down during digestion. It plays an important role in keeping your digestive system in working order and may reduce the risk of some types of cancer, heart disease and Type 2 diabetes. Fiber comes in two forms—insoluble (whole-grain products such as wheat bran cereal, vegetables and fruit)—and soluble (peas, beans, oat bran, whole grains, barley, cereals, seeds, rice, crackers, many vegetables and fruits and some pasta and other bakery products).

Total Fat represents the combined fats that provide energy to the body. Some types of fat are healthier than others. Saturated fat is a type of fat that is solid at room temperature. It is usually animal based and is associated with certain health risks. Trans fat is created when liquid fat is turned into solid fat during manufacturing. It has no food value and should be replaced with unsaturated fat whenever possible. Unsaturated fat is a type of fat that is liquid at room temperature and is typically plant based. Examples are: olive, canola, soy, corn, sunflower, peanut and nut oils. You can also get your good fats in nuts, seeds, avocados and fatty fish, notably cold-water fish like salmon, sardines and mackerel.

Carbohydrates are your body's main source of energy and aid in the production of serotonin, which facilitates a happy, stable mood. They also aid in sleep and help curb food cravings and depression. Without this macronutrient, the brain can't properly function, blood sugar becomes unstable and neurotransmitters become disrupted. Complex carbohydrates (green vegetables, fresh fruits, beans and nuts) are better for you than simple carbohydrates (refined and processed junk food) and release energy over a longer period of time. Refined breads, candy and sugary cereal and "diet" drinks and desserts are merely a "quick fix" and turn to fat more quickly.

Omega-3 fatty acid consumption may help with depression by assisting in the uptake of neurotransmitters and decreasing inflammation. Having a proper balance of omega-6 and omega-3 fatty acids helps neurotransmitter receptors function, which in turn helps increase the amount of neurotransmitters that can be active in the brain. Research is showing benefits for cognitive capacities across a lifespan in addition to reduction of aggression and symptoms of ADHD and depressive disorders. The protein in fish and shellfish comes with the benefit of omega-3 fatty acids, reported to decrease the risk of coronary artery disease. Supplements containing polyunsaturated fatty acids have been recommended to help reduce anxiety in people with substance abuse.

The average American consumes about 22 teaspoons of sugar a day. Research finds that excess sugar can increase blood pressure, lower "good" HDL cholesterol levels and increase your risk of heart disease, diabetes and obesity. Keep high-sugar candy bars, cookies and other foods to a minimum. They don't contain the nutrition you need, and only give you energy for a short while. Sugary baked goods and "energy" bars can spoil your appetite for healthier meals. Instead, have an apple, some berries or a grapefruit. Their sugars are absorbed slowly.

Sugar hides in white bread, white rice and white pasta. Your best alternatives are whole grains and steel-cut oats. Also, one glass of juice has as much sugar as several pieces of fruit, but no fiber to slow absorption. Opt for eating whole fruit over drinking juice.

Keep your body hydrated for clear thinking and better performance. Drink six to eight cups of water a day. Soda, energy drinks and coffee don't count as healthy liquids. Limit your caffeine intake to no more than 3 or 4 cups (8 oz. each) a day. Decaffeinated coffee has about 3% of a regular cup of coffee, so you may want to try that as a substitute.

Possible Actions for Implementation

- Eat slowly to give the brain time to register that hunger is satisfied.

- Drink lots of liquids throughout your day (water, herbal or green tea, coconut water or green juice).

- Eat between five and nine servings of fruits and vegetables every day (fresh or frozen).

- Choose whole grain bread and cereal. Eliminate cereals with added sugar.

- Use less salt, sugar and saturated fat.

- Eat more beans and grains.

- Reduce servings of red meat and processed meats, such as bacon, deli/luncheon meats, hot dogs.

- Choose organic milk and cheeses if possible.

- Choose lean meats, poultry and fish.

- Stick to regular mealtimes.

- Get more protein, complex carbohydrates, and dietary fiber.

- Vitamin and mineral supplements (B-complex, zinc, and vitamins A & C) may be helpful during recovery.

Now that you know what to eat and why, let's talk about knowing what's in the food you buy and serving sizes.

Most store-bought food is in a package with nutritional composition on the back of the package. Understanding what the Nutrition Facts Label includes can help you make food choices that are best for your health and recovery. Here are the basics you should know:

1. **Serving Size** - These are given in familiar measurements such as cups or pieces. This section shows how many servings are in the package, and how big the serving is. It is common for a food package to contain more than one serving, so read carefully.

2. **Calorie Count** - Calorie content shows how many calories there are in one serving. A product that's fat-free, for example, isn't necessarily calorie free. Read the label to see how many calories are in one serving of the food.

3. **Percent (%) Daily Value** - Based on a 2,000-calorie diet, this section tells you how the nutrients in one serving contribute to your total daily diet. Use it to choose foods that are high in the nutrients you should get more of, and low in the nutrients you want less of. Your nutritional needs largely depend on how physically active you are. Talk with your healthcare provider to see what calorie level is right for you.

Meal planning is essential. Here are some examples of healthy breakfast and snack choices:

Breakfast Ideas
- Fresh fruit, yogurt, whole wheat toast or muffin
- Fresh fruit, whole wheat bagel with peanut butter, milk
- Eggs as you like them, with fruit and whole wheat toast

Snack Ideas
- Fresh fruit
- Small handful of almonds
- Yogurt
- Crackers and cheese
- A piece of lean meat on a piece of whole wheat bread
- Almond butter on celery

Describe what you think are healthy lunch and dinner choices and share these ideas with your group or support person:

Lunch Menu:

_____

_____

_____

_____

_____

_____

_____

Dinner Menu:

_____

_____

_____

_____

_____

_____

Name several of your favorite snacks and one of your favorite meals:

_____

_____

_____

_____

_____

How would you rate them in terms of nutrition?

_____

_____

_____

_____

_____

_____

Here is a summary of the steps to healthy eating:

1. Make good nutrition part of everyday living.

2. Eat well at home, work and play: 50% veggies and fruit, 25% whole grains and 25% meat, poultry, fish or other sources of protein.

3. Quit the Clean Plate Club; eat for nutrition, not out of boredom, anger or depression.

4. Don't drink your calories (sugar-laden colas, milkshakes, high-calorie sports drinks).

5. Avoid so-called "energy" drinks.

Your Ideas

Name five things you can do this week to start eating better:

_____

_____

_____

_____

_____

_____

_____

Make a meal plan for a whole week. Write it in the pages in Appendix. Then make a grocery list to match your meal plan.

Grocery List:

_____

_____

_____

_____

_____

Benefits of Good Nutrition

- Healthy heart
- Strong bones and teeth
- Higher energy levels
- Brain health
- Healthy weight
- Decreased cancer risk
- Blood sugar control
- Anti-aging
- Stronger immune system
- Improved mood
- Better skin tone

Unfortunately, large corporations have taken over much of our food supply in the last several decades. Our most nutritious food is to be found at farmer's markets and small groceries. These may not be as convenient as large supermarkets, but it is worth your time and effort to shop carefully, ask questions and read labels. Whenever possible, support organic farmers and those who raise and kill animals humanely.

CHAPTER 2

Exercise: We Are Designed to Move

*Aerobic exercise is healthful, inexpensive and insufficiently
utilized for a variety of psychiatric disorders.*
—Harvard Medical Letter

The Reasons Why

Exercise is a key to mental health. Our bodies are mechanical miracles that enable us to walk, run, lift and play. As we use them, our bodies adapt and flourish. Our muscles grow stronger, our bones tougher, our hearts more powerful. Health improves as we become leaner and fitter and less likely to develop chronic diseases, such as diabetes, obesity, high blood pressure or cancer.

Exercise benefits the brain and mind. We know that the brain is amazingly responsive and can even increase in size when stimulated by exercise or meditation, or when fed a healthy diet. When we walk or work out, more blood and oxygen flow to the brain and over time, new blood vessels form and the new blood vessels become permanent. Any kind of movement is good, but, according to research, vigorous exercise for 30 minutes regularly is especially helpful.

Human beings were made to move. Exercise offers you both preventative and therapeutic psychological benefits. While it is obvious that your feelings can influence your movement, you may not know that your movement can impact your feelings, too. For example, when you feel tired and sad, you tend to move more slowly. When you feel anxious, you may rush around or be stuck, frozen. Research shows that the connection between your brain and your body is a two-way street, and that means that movement can change your brain, too.

Exercise and recreation provide opportunities to get away from it all, and to either enjoy some solitude or make friends and build support networks.

Teens beginning a program of recovery must tend to the body first. If alcoholism or addiction has caused your body to become deconditioned and your immune system to be weakened. a well thought-out, planned exercise program begins the process of rebuilding both.

Make a note here about your current level of fitness. What kind of shape is your body in?

_____

_____

_____

_____

_____

_____

The mental benefits of exercise have a neurochemical basis. Movement reduces levels of the body's stress hormones, such as adrenaline and cortisol. It also stimulates the production of endorphins, chemicals in the brain that are the body's natural painkillers and mood elevators. When you excrcise, your body boosts critical brain chemicals—dopamine, noradrenaline, and serotonin, which create a natural high. These chemicals, which your brain associates with rewarding behaviors, give you feelings of wellbeing and relaxation that you may have only gotten in the past through substance abuse.

However, abuse of drugs and alcohol causes an imbalance that eventually interferes with your ability to feel pleasure, happiness, and satisfaction. Dedicated physical activity helps you reintroduce natural levels of endorphins into your system. This not only helps you feel better, but also re-teaches your body that it is capable of regulating its own brain chemistry and mood in healthy, natural ways.

Have you noticed the feelings of relaxation and optimism that accompany a hard workout—or the hot shower after your exercise is over? This is due to a release of endorphins, the "feel-good" hormones. Regular exercise makes your brain's "fight or flight" system less reactive, and keeps you calmer longer. Elite athletes say exercise keeps their moods stable. And, they are not the only ones! It appears true that regular aerobic exercise, in many cases, may be just as effective as antidepressants. It's also cheaper, with fewer side effects.

In addition to the chemical changes happening in your brain when you exercise, working out can reduce the negative effects of giving up your substance(s) or behavior(s), which may include sleep troubles, anxiety, depression and weight gain. Simply by improving your overall health and wellbeing, regular exercise rebuilds your body and your immune system, and gives you a healthy way to release difficult or pent-up emotions, including anger, sadness and frustration.

When you are anxious or fearful, you may experience a rapid heartbeat and have trouble focusing and concentrating. Exercise can focus your thoughts, increase your energy and reduce feelings of confusion, fatigue and depression. In the Meditation section of this workbook, you will learn how the meditative movement of qigong, tai chi or yoga can reduce stress as well as provide exercise for the body. Changing your posture, breathing and rhythm can change your brain, reducing stress, depression and anxiety and leading to general feelings of wellbeing.

Through movement, you can refocus your thoughts on your wellbeing and forget, at least briefly, whatever else is going on in your life. You may leave your workout with a clearer mind, feeling more rejuvenated and optimistic. Finding this clarity within chaos can make recovery more sustainable.

You don't need to be a fitness fanatic or marathoner to reap the benefits of exercise, but you do need to develop a routine. Making fitness part of every day can help stave off cravings, reduce stress and avoid major illnesses.

You can exercise by yourself or with others. Meet a friend in the morning for a walk or sign up for a class at the Y or a local gym. Exercising with someone else can boost how you feel about yourself and relationships. When you synchronize your movement with others, studies indicate that you like them more and feel more charitable toward them. That's probably why dance therapy can help depression and anxiety. Your mind and body are intimately connected. While your brain is the master control system for your body's movement, the way you move can also affect the way you think and feel. Having a regularly scheduled time to devote to exercise can help when you need to de-stress or retreat to have time for yourself.

When you are too exhausted to use thought-control strategies, such as focusing on the positive or looking at a troubling situation from a different perspective, movement can come to the rescue. Working out, going on a meditative walk by yourself or going for a walk with someone else can help you feel better.

Nothing is quick and easy, but with the right attitude and goals in mind, you will enjoy the journey you are undertaking. It has worked for countless others, and it can work for you. If you are not as strong as you'd like to be, understand that the physical benefits come with time, but the mental and emotional perks of exercise happen right away. So, make it happen for you!

Possible Actions for Implementation

YOU are all you need to start and continue a successful exercise program. You don't need to invest in an expensive health club membership or have the latest athletic wear or high-tech equipment. If you have floor space, try simple floor exercises. You can get in shape with many different types of training or activities, and YouTube is filled with exercise routines if you don't know where to begin. Type in "Exercise for Beginners," and a menu of possibilities will pop up.

Many cities have free classes, maps of walking trails and bird-watching sites, fitness parks and bike trails. Does your high school or college have a pool, tennis courts or running tracks? There are televised fitness shows, downloadable exercise regimens and so much more.

You may want to work with a personal trainer or experienced buddy who can help you stay motivated and challenged during the early weeks of training. You'll want to do things correctly to prevent injury and discouragement. Be sure that your exercise program is appropriately varied to include strength training, aerobics, flexibility and core training. Typically, you will need to move your body fast enough to get your heart rate to a maximum number of beats per minute (220 minus your age). No matter what your current fitness level, committing to a regular exercise program and getting some type of physical activity most days of the week, is an incredibly effective way to support your recovery.

The most important thing is that you like what you're doing and that you are willing to be a little adventurous. Try not to focus on perfection or what others can do. Focus instead on increasing your healthy behavior. Make it a habit to walk 15 minutes a day, and add time, distance and intensity from there. Remember, everyone starts somewhere. So, if you are already a devoted exerciser, keep it up. If you are new to a regular exercise regimen, just get started. And if you encounter your own resistance, please know that this is common. We are creatures of habit, and getting a new habit in place can be challenging. But it is doable, so don't give up!

Before getting started, let's talk about your resistance, if you have any. Please write down the reasons you think you can't add exercise to your daily life.

_____

_____

_____

_____

_____

_____

_____

Now write about what you might do to overcome your resistance. By the way, resistance is normal. Our ancestors tried to avoid expending energy. So much energy was involved in survival that they did not have to plan exercise; it was automatic and essential. Often, that resistance and avoidance is built into our DNA.

_____

_____

_____

_____

_____

_____

Think of the ways you can add exercise to your daily routine. You can participate in brisk walking, playing a sport, doing yoga or working out at the gym. You can combine these activities into a routine that changes from day to day, if you like. You need to exercise at least three times a week for 30 minutes at a time to provide valuable physical improvement. If you want to experience cognitive benefits, you'll need to combine strength training with aerobics to achieve more strenuous exercise.

You will begin to see benefits within a month of regular physical activity, and will likely notice that your mood is better and more stable and you are more energetic. Importantly, you'll also have the satisfaction of knowing you're doing something for yourself and your wellbeing. These benefits increase over the course of six months.

Write down some ideas you have to add a regular exercise routine to your week. If you already have a routine, write down what you do and where you see there could be improvement.

_____

_____

_____

_____

_____

It goes without saying that you should speak with your healthcare advisor before beginning any sort of exercise program. When you have the okay, here are some ideas about how to begin.

Except during illness, you should exercise nearly every day to stay healthy and reduce stress. That doesn't necessarily mean training for a marathon or swimming laps, but it does mean:

- 30 to 40 minutes of moderate exercise, such as walking, or 15 to 20 minutes of vigorous exercise
- Walking at least two miles a day, or the equivalent amount of another activity: You can do it all at once or in 10- to 15-minute chunks if that fits your schedule better.
- Adding on a little strength training and stretching two to three times a week
- Including deep breathing or muscle relaxation exercises, especially if you need more help with stress.

Any type of physical activity can be transformed into an exercise routine and, before long, all the fun you have translates into tremendous health benefits.

WAYS TO GET A WORKOUT

- Walking for fitness
- Running/jogging
- Treadmill
- Aerobics classes
- Stairmaster
- Rowing
- Yoga
- Tennis
- Racquet ball
- Marathons or triathlons
- Pilates
- Kickboxing
- Free weights, hand weights
- Bicycling
- Tai chi
- Weight/resistance machines
- Weight training
- Stretching
- Swimming
- Standup paddle boarding
- Shuffleboard
- Bocce ball

Hiking/walking – A simple 30-minute walk outdoors can stave off cravings and also boost overall brain function by supporting new brain cell growth.

Strength training – Weight training or body-weight exercises like push-ups can help reboot the body's sleep cycle and relieve insomnia.

Team sports – Throwing the ball, shooting some hoops or cycling with other people will provide more than a good workout. The social interaction with friends or like-minded people will help you replace old, unhealthy activities with new, healthy ones. Exercising outdoors in the company of others allows you to check the boxes on three of the *8 Ways to Sustainable Wellbeing*. It's not about having to train hard or train long. It's more about just getting out there and moving.

Obstacle courses, rock-climbing walls and ropes courses are physical challenges that can boost your self-confidence as dopamine is released in your brain. The memories made during these exercises can be strong reminders that you're capable of overcoming any hurdle.

Set realistic goals and timelines. All significant life changes take patience and commitment in practicing the new principles and skills. Use your support system to surround yourself with exercise buddies, coaches or workout buddies to help you stick to your plan. Stop comparing yourself to other people who are in fantastic shape and focus on your own efforts, endurance and changes. Recognize your accomplishments, beginning with just getting up and moving. It all counts.

Behavioral factors contribute to the emotional benefits you'll experience. As your strength and stamina increase, your self-image will improve. You'll earn a sense of mastery and control, pride and self-confidence. Your renewed vigor and energy will help you succeed in many tasks, and the discipline of regular exercise will help you achieve your lifestyle goals. Enjoy feelings of accomplishment, pride and self-worth as you reach benchmarks in your long-term goals. Denial and delay are enemies of the new you. Get started today, with just a walk around the block. Eliminate the usual excuses: no time, not the right shoes, no exercise clothes, too tired, no one to exercise with, etc. If you hate the gym, try dancing, tennis, walking, home exercise programs or gardening instead. **Realize that exercise is part of relapse prevention.**

There is another benefit that is not talked about much, but that is important, and that is that long-term muscle tension leads to what is called muscle armor tension patterns. The body becomes habituated to being in a tense posture, which is unhealthy. Flexibility is lost and the rigidity of the muscles leads to chronic pain. Regular exercise, as well as deep tissue massage, may help release this muscle armor and create more flexibility and reduce chronic pain.

As with anything new you learn, the more you do it, the better you get. If you have been inactive for a while as a result of depression or too much time on screens, start with a simple walking program, and gradually increase the frequency or length of your walks as you feel stronger. Add more intensity to your regimen and you'll realize the physical and mental health benefits and feel more competent in your ability to meet the challenges you will face in recovery. Following these guidelines and consistently applying the knowledge you've gained will give you lifelong satisfaction.

Your Ideas

This week, schedule 30 minutes of physical movement for at least three days and add more days if you can.

	Day, Date, Time	Exercise
Day 1		
Day 2		
Day 3		
Day 4		
Day 5		
Day 6		
Day 7		

Now make some notes about what worked and what didn't. What, if anything, needs new planning to make your routine sustainable?

_____

_____

_____

_____

_____

_____

_____

_____

_____

_____

_____

_____

_____

_____

_____

_____

_____

_____

_____

_____

_____

_____

_____

_____

_____

_____

_____

Now, see what you can do to keep your momentum going. Use the charts in the Appendix to keep track of your exercise. Remember, the research says that people who chart their progress, using check marks, gold stars or whatever little "reward" they like, actually do better at sustaining the habit they are trying to integrate into their routine.

Benefits of Regular Exercise

- Improves mood and sense of wellbeing
- Adds structure, which makes life more manageable, so recovery is more sustainable
- Increases energy, improves sleep and overall health
- Improves cognitive function to support finding clarity within chaos
- Helps prevent and heal disorders such as addiction, anxiety and depression
- Improves immune function
- Improves cholesterol
- Reduces blood sugar
- Reduces the risk of heart attack, stroke, colon and breast cancers, osteoporosis and fractures
- Reduces chronic pain
- Improves flexibility, balance and agility
- Releases endorphins that create pleasurable feelings
- Enhances self-efficacy and self esteem
- Interrupts negative thoughts
- Releases chronic psychosomatic muscle tension
- Aids in sweating toxins out of the body
- Improves muscle strength
- Improves circulation
- Sharpens mental skills, including executive functioning
- Improves body image
- Improves flow of oxygen and respiratory functioning

Exercise is something that most everyone can do in some form. You don't have to be an elite athlete to take a walk in your neighborhood in the morning and evening. The natural anti-anxiety and mood-elevation properties of exercise may take a while to be noticeable, so keep at it. Make exercise a daily enterprise. You'll be glad you did.

CHAPTER 3

Relaxation: Breathe In, Breathe Out...Aaah

Mindfulness is the single most powerful tool available
for those seeking freedom from addiction.
—Tara Brach, Ph.D., author of *Radical Acceptance*

The Reasons Why

Practicing relaxation through mindfulness, stillness, silence and attention will change your life. The benefits of relaxation are endless in our world that values overstimulation, and where we see more people, often travel further daily and encounter sensory overstimulation of every sort more frequently than our ancestors did in a lifetime. Though we humans were really not made for this sort of speed and the constant decision-making and pressure that it requires, it has now become the norm. There really is no way to avoid it altogether outside of entering a monastery or other means of withdrawing from the world. Therefore, we all need ways to quiet the mind and relax the body.

According to Dr. Walsh's research, we need a time of quiet, a time with few, if any, distractions, a time for just being in the present moment. This is the essence of what is often called mindfulness meditation. The healing and soothing practice of spending deliberate time quieting the mind, reducing sensory stimuli and practicing mindfulness will give you peace and serenity. This quiet and mindful awareness cultivates rest and insight. The famed German psychiatrist Victor Frankl said, "Between stimulus and response, there is a space. In that space is our power to choose our response. In our response lies our growth and freedom."

Often, recovering teens need more time between a stimulus, such as, "I want to get high," and a response, such as, "I think I'll call a recovery friend instead." Learning mindfulness is a good way to begin to have that pause that Dr. Frankl was referring to.

In this chapter, you will learn suggested ways of coping with the demands of a busy life, as well as techniques to prevent relapse in recovery through relaxation and mindfulness. These practices will help you to:

1. Realize the potential of self-direction (as opposed to "going along to get along")
2. Assume personal responsibility as a major factor in health and sickness
3. Minimize detrimental effects of stress and distress
4. Achieve and maintain a high level of wellbeing
5. Improve impulse control, so vital to recovering teens.

The stress of everyday life and the work of maintaining your recovery can undermine your wellbeing on many levels. Even though stress is universal, few teens—or adults, for that matter—are trained in managing it. Therefore, many people respond self-destructively—aided by the ever-present, unhealthy influence of advertising, celebrity "role models" and availability of drugs and alcohol—to cope with pressure and temptation. Temporary fixes are just that—temporary—often leaving you feeling worse or causing more problems. Learning tools for stress management is essential to living your life plan and achieving both short-term and long-term goals.

We have identified four forms of stress: 1) behavioral stress when we are physically challenged or exhausted, 2) emotional stress when our feelings have been hurt or upset in some way, 3) intellectual stress when we have been stretching our capacity for learning new material and 4) psychological stress when our values or beliefs are challenged. Stress can be either acute or chronic. Acute stress is a response to a current significant challenge. Chronic stress, by comparison, is ongoing and produces a constant state of anxious arousal. By learning mindfulness meditation techniques, as well as other methods for improved coping, teens can use stress constructively to promote good health and self-development.

It is a fact that people who are susceptible to addiction and relapse from addiction tend to be stress sensitive, meaning that they are especially sensitive to one or more of the types of stress previously identified. When teens have learned new ways of coping with stressful situations, their sense of self-efficacy—your belief that you can succeed—will be strengthened and the probability of relapse will be decreased. One of the most potent and readily accessible coping mechanisms we have at our disposal is mindfulness meditation.

G. Alan Marlatt, Ph.D., wrote, "One of the most significant effects of regular meditation practice is the development of mindfulness: the capacity to observe the ongoing process of experience without at the same time becoming 'attached' or identifying with the content of each thought, feeling, or image. Mindfulness is a particularly effective cognitive skill in relapse prevention. If clients can acquire this ability through the regular practice of meditation, they may be able to 'detach' themselves from the lure of urges, cravings, or cognitive rationalizations that may otherwise lead to a lapse."

We all have urges and cravings, and our rationale for indulging ourselves in these. Dr. Marlatt is saying that in order to avoid giving in to the urges and cravings that are a part of recovery, we need a means of counteracting them that enhances recovery and our overall functioning. He says that, in his experience, mindfulness meditation is just such a means and a tool.

Please note in the space provided some of the stresses that stimulate urges and cravings in you.

_____

_____

_____

_____

_____

_____

It's important to note that stress is the product of an entire lifestyle, not just the product of an occasional crisis, death of a loved one, argument, disturbing news, high-stimulus situations or road rage. Consequently, monitoring your internal arousal level is important—meaning, how anxious do you feel at any given time or in general? Stress management is a skill we must each develop, because *coping* cannot be delegated to someone else; it must be internalized as a part of our personal makeup.

Have you had experience with relaxation through mindfulness or meditation? Please write about your experience and your willingness to participate in this form of relaxation at this time.

_____

_____

_____

_____

_____

_____

It's important to learn to identify your stress signals in order to prevent tensions from building up and ultimately losing control over your choices and behavior. You can learn to reduce your tensions before they are anything more than a clenched jaw or a quickened pulse. You can be that relaxed person whose honesty, ability to reflect and self-acceptance keeps you in charge of yourself.

For some, stress is no more than anxiety or physical nervousness, but for others, stress can lead to despair and mental illness. Making a conscious effort to be aware of the physical signs that mean your body is anticipating "fight, flight or freeze" is an important part of stress reduction. We get physical hints of what is to come before it happens, if we pay attention and catch the signs early. Some possible early warning signals might be:

- Rapid breathing
- Sweaty palms
- Butterflies in the stomach
- Racing heart
- Perspiration
- Muscular tension
- Feelings of unhappiness and/or depression
- An overabundance of nervous energy.

What happens for you when you are overly stressed?

_____

_____

_____

_____

_____

_____

What do you usually do to relax and de-stress?

_____

_____

_____

_____

_____

_____

Recovering teens often experience considerable guilt and shame about their past behavior. These are challenging emotions to cope with and can, in and of themselves, lead to relapse. For that reason, it's important to keep your eye on the present moment and have a means of transforming these thoughts into actions that shift the energy from negative to positive. Therefore, establishing a mindfulness practice that keeps you in the present moment, as well as other relaxation techniques, is essential to long-term recovery.

John Kabat-Zinn defined mindfulness as "a way of paying attention on purpose, in the present moment, and nonjudgmentally." When we can see and experience things as they are in the present moment, instead of dwelling endlessly on the regrets of the past, or our anxiety and worry about the future or where the next fix is coming from, we begin to have agency in directing our lives in meaningful and thoughtful ways.

In addition, recovery emphasizes acknowledging, feeling and experiencing upsets and discomfort when they arise—not trying to escape these feelings, but rather learning to tolerate them as passing and mostly temporary experiences that we all have. It's likely that you have heard the maxim, "Pause when agitated," in 12-Step meetings, and it's good advice. Mindfulness emphasizes that those circumstances, whether physical, environmental, emotional or psychological, are changing all the time, and as the Bible says, "This, too, shall pass."

Though we are emphasizing a mindfulness meditation practice, you probably have discovered some other healthy ways to relax. In the space below, write some examples of healthy ways in which you typically kick back and relax.

_____

_____

_____

Possible Actions for Implementation

If you have trouble thinking about what to do to unwind, here are some suggestions:

- Go for a walk
- Take some time out and focus on what's happening around you
- Listen to quiet and relaxing music
- Go fishing
- Take a bath
- Go to a movie or watch a DVD
- Focus your attention on a puzzle
- Read a book
- Do yoga
- Repeat affirmations
- Breathe in, counting to four; hold for four counts; and exhale for a count of four.
- Take time to develop or continue a hobby
- Color in a coloring book.

We recommend mindfulness meditation as a daily practice for relaxation and optimizing mental health. Ask your parent, therapist or other knowledgeable person to help you find a teacher, and stay with the teacher until you have established your own sustainable practice.

Start by setting aside 10 minutes a day to sit quietly with eyes closed or lowered. Place your feet on the floor and hands palms up and open on your lap. Get comfortable. Choose a word or a brief prayer or affirmation to repeat silently. Or you can count your breaths, breathing slowly and deeply, so that you can feel the rise and fall of your belly. Set a quiet timer ahead of time so that you don't have to worry about when to end. Typically, your mind will wander. No judging … just gently bring your mind back to the word(s) you have chosen, or to silence. You may be surprised at how difficult this is if you are a beginner. But, in time, you will begin to look forward to this quiet recharging of your energy.

When you have done this three times on three different days, write about your experience (easy/hard, boring/interesting, relaxing/tense, etc.).

_____

_____

_____

_____

_____

_____

It can be helpful to begin your mindfulness practice by using a CD or smartphone app to get you started. There are seemingly endless CDs and apps available; Headspace and Calm are two of the most popular. Try out several of them and see what you like. But, like anything else, it only works if you do it consistently.

There has been much written about mindfulness meditation for relaxation, and this is a chapter that could be a book in itself. But, for our purposes here, the idea is to set aside a time each day for mindfulness meditation for relaxation. The goal is to begin with 5–10 minutes of silence, when you are focused on your breathing and using the word or phrase that you have chosen to help you stay present with your breathing. Hopefully, this will extend to 20, 30 or more minutes each day over time. You will be pleased with the results and rewarded with the benefits.

Your Ideas

What is the best time in your regular day to set aside for mindfulness meditation practice?

_____

_____

Who or what will help you to maintain this practice until it can become a habit?

_____

_____

The key principle of a more relaxed approach to life is balance—arranging your life in such a way that your needs are fulfilled in healthy proportion and you don't become overloaded with any of the experiences or events that produce intolerable stress and lead to relapse.

This workbook takes a synergistic approach to healing and wellness. That is, the combined action of the eight areas of wellbeing produce a balance of many dimensions of living and working in order to achieve a quality of life that is productive, nurturing and satisfying. What you do in one area supports, enhances and capitalizes on actions in the others. Conversely, if one or more aspects of your life are unattended to or awry, your equilibrium is thrown off balance, often with unfavorable results. Know that wellness is an attainable goal for you. It takes practice, but the rewards are worth it.

On a related note, one important way to reduce stress is something indigenous people call "shape shifting." Shape shifting means shifting the energy or your point of view about the challenging situation. For example, if something or someone is bothering or upsetting you, say to yourself, "There is another way to see this (person/situation)." Then, ask yourself, "What is another way to see this person or situation?" When you are able to change your view or perception of the situation, you have shape-shifted it. We are not talking about denying what is, but rather changing your point of view to one that is more positive and useful.

Just as a slight shift in the tilt of a kaleidoscope changes the whole design you see, a small change in your point of view of a person or situation will provide you with relief and a less stressful way of seeing it. This is a powerful stress-reduction technique.

Describe a situation that you would like to shape shift.

_____

_____

_____

_____

_____

Now describe another way you could see this that would not be false, but would shift the energy to something more positive and less stressful.

_____

_____

_____

_____

_____

_____

Your stress response is individual to your life experiences and mental and physical state. Responses can span a spectrum from regression and disability, to resilience and normal functioning, to growth and strength. Three basic coping techniques are:

1. Managing the number of stressors you encounter by controlling the pace of your life
2. Fortifying your stress filter through physical and mental conditioning to reduce the harmful effects of stressful events
3. Channeling your stress responses into positive attitudes and behaviors (shape-shifting) and personal effectiveness.

What causes you the most noticeable stress? List the top 10 triggers that make you uncomfortable, reduce your functioning and/or cause you to be tempted to relapse or behave badly. They can be people, situations, times, places, events, moments, goings or comings. Take your time to think of incidents when you lost control and acted out.

My Top 10 Triggers (Write down who was involved, what happened, why, where, when and how you acted.)

1. _____

_____

_____

_____

_____

2. _____

_____

_____

_____

_____

3. _____

_____

_____

_____

_____

4. _____

_____

_____

_____

_____

5. _____

_____

_____

_____

_____

6. _____

_____

_____

_____

_____

7. _____

_____

_____

_____

_____

8. _____

_____

_____

_____

_____

_____

9. _____

_____

_____

_____

_____

_____

10. _____

_____

_____

_____

_____

_____

Using mindfulness meditation and other relaxation techniques for stress management is important for mental health. Stress can make your body adapt and become stronger, and it can even be good when it pushes you to learn new skills, stretch your limits or reach new levels of mastery and success—in short, to thrive. Make the distinction between *distress* and *eustress.* Distress causes you to feel upset or overwhelmed. Eustress is the excitement and pressure that comes from competition that you choose to engage in, for example. It's the positive reaction to the stress that generates within you a desire to achieve and overcome a challenge. So, it is your perceptions of a stressor, to some degree, that determine if you are feeling distress or eustress.

When it is severe or chronic, unrelieved stress can exact a toll on both body and mind. Mentally, it can become anxiety and depression. Physically, it can cause adrenal failure or other medical crises.

This is where your mindfulness meditation practice comes into play. Having a daily practice is like putting money in a savings account for unexpected expenses. When unexpected stresses occur, you will have enough resources in the "bank" to manage the situation without being triggered into relapse.

There are many ways you can keep stress under control in your life. As you are learning in this workbook, exercise, health-enhancing recreation, good nutrition, positive relationships and spiritual practice will all benefit you. Coloring books and puzzles with tranquil scenes or elegant patterns are also good ways to slow down.

Movement is a great stress-management strategy when it is rhythmic in nature and performed slowly. Walking meditation, tai chi, qi gong, reading for pleasure and other TLCs can be relaxing. Yoga offers both somatic (body) and contemplative (mind) benefits. Along with meditation, it has been shown to enhance various psychological capacities, health and maturity. Focused meditation is one of the most direct ways to activate and strengthen those areas in the brain that increase empathy, which is one reason we emphasize it in this chapter.

Muscle relaxation therapies that require you to systematically tighten and then relax major muscle groups can be beneficial, too, particularly in treating panic and generalized anxiety. Try muscle contractions before bed: Before you fall asleep, scan through your body, tensing each muscle group—squeezing it—and then relaxing it. Start all the way at your toes and work up your body to the crown of your head.

You can also practice deep breathing; throughout the day, take a moment to take a couple of deep breaths. Breathe in through the nose for a count of four and out through the nose for a count of eight.

Try deep breathing for two minutes right now and note your experience.

_____

_____

_____

_____

_____

_____

_____

_____

Remember that relaxation, physical rest, meditation and mindfulness are all interconnected. The more you practice, the better you will get at these things. It takes a while to establish the practice, so don't get discouraged. Stick with it. You will become good at it and your quality of life will leap forward.

Benefits of Relaxation

- Slows your heart rate
- Lowers blood pressure
- Slows your breathing rate
- Reduces activity of stress hormones
- Increases blood flow to major muscles
- Reduces muscle tension and chronic pain
- Reduces depression
- Reduces anxiety
- Improves concentration and mood
- Improves sleep
- Helps reduce chronic headaches and other types of chronic pain
- Lowers fatigue

In the chart on the next page, log your date and time of practicing mindfulness meditation or other techniques for relaxation.

Date	Time Spent	Practice Technique

CHAPTER 4
Recreation: Fun Is Fun-damental

Sometimes the inessential is essential!
—T. L. Reese

The Reasons Why

Recreation, humor and play not only feel good, but also do us good. Playfulness is built into our biology, as we can see in most species—puppies, kittens, monkeys and children. Children's play is more than having fun. It is a way of experimenting, expanding limits, training muscles and developing minds. Play is a way of learning to live together, learning how to compete and cooperate, to make friends and acquire social skills. It's fun, but also an integral part of learning and growing. It's the same for teens and adults, and it is a critical aspect of a healthy lifestyle.

Leisure is your discretionary time spent in non-compulsory activities, time spent away from obligations, cares, school and/or work. Because leisure time is free from these compulsory activities, such as employment, household chores, school and other such day-to-day activities (not including eating and sleeping), it is often referred to as "free time." For teens, down time is beneficial for refreshing and revitalizing yourself. You speed up our recovery from the stresses of school or work, reduce painful emotions and foster feelings of happiness and joy. It is a fact that laughter is good medicine!

Involvement in enjoyable activities is central to your healthy lifestyle, and hopefully brings feelings of freedom and joy. Through experiences of positive emotions, we can transform ourselves, becoming more creative, knowledgeable, resilient, socially integrated and healthy individuals. Research indicates that recreation, often synonymous with play, is something that is hardwired in our biology. You just have to find ways to do it that you enjoy, but that do not interfere with or jeopardize your hard-won recovery.

How to have fun and enjoy free time in recovery is often a big challenge and question mark for recovering teens. So many leisure activities that teens in recovery have enjoyed in the past have been paired with partying—drinking or using their drug(s) of choice—that to engage in those same activities without drinking alcohol or using drugs seems odd or boring at best, and a trigger for relapse at worst. For teens, partying is considered to be an activity in and of itself … and it was probably fun, until it became destructive and dangerous.

There is something called state-dependent learning, which is a phenomenon in which memory retrieval is most efficient when the person is in the same state of consciousness as they were when the memory was formed. For example, this means that if you have only ever danced while drunk or high, you might not remember how to do it very well in your sober state. You may have to start over to learn to dance, and suffer the awkwardness of being a beginner again. Likewise, if you enjoy music and going to concerts, you may find that going to the same concerts that you attended pre-recovery are not as enjoyable as you had remembered. This means that things that you found fun, entertaining or easy in the past may not be so now.

This may not be universally true for all recovering teens engaging in activities that previously gave them pleasure, but it is true often enough to come to the attention of therapists and sponsors working with them. Even something as pleasurable as sexual activity may have to be relearned in your sober state. So, please don't be alarmed about not quite knowing what to do for fun and pleasure. This is a common problem for recovering teens.

Recreation includes any activities that you find enjoyable, that help you have fun and be adventurous, that challenge you and give you a needed break from everyday responsibilities. It is time out from taking care of the necessities of life, time for engaging in personally gratifying pursuits.

Recreation in sobriety may require you to try some new activities that you might not have considered in the past. Not only is this a good idea from the standpoint of expanding your repertoire of possible ways to spend free time, but it is also important from the standpoint of letting go of activities that you have typically done while drinking or using.

What are some of the activities in which you engaged in the past that you associate with drinking or using? List them on the next page.

_____

_____

_____

_____

_____

_____

Have you noticed any activities that you engaged in pre-recovery that now feel awkward or uninteresting to you? Describe them here.

_____

_____

_____

_____

_____

Has this caused any problems for you? If so, what sort of problems?

_____

_____

_____

_____

_____

_____

_____

Do any of these activities that used to be fun and now feel challenging (because you aren't as good at them or don't find them as pleasurable) seem worth doing again, with some relearning about how to do them while sober?

_____

_____

_____

_____

_____

Either way, please explain.

_____

_____

_____

_____

_____

Give some examples of what makes you laugh.

_____

_____

_____

_____

_____

_____

_____

What do you do that makes other people laugh?

_____

_____

_____

_____

_____

_____

_____

Possible Actions for Implementation

The world is an enormous place with a zillion things, activities, people, places, etc. to be interested in and take pleasure in. So, just know that when you have free time and don't really know what to do with yourself, it is time for exploration. The following possibilities are just a few of an endless list of things that might interest you and give you the recreation (literally re-creation), fun and time out that is essential to good mental health and recovery.

If you see something on this list that is a possible interest or activity, circle it for future exploration.

1. Team sports – There are leagues for bowling, indoor and outdoor soccer, softball, baseball, hockey, swimming and just about every other team sport there is. Investigate and sign up.

2. Individual sports – Archery, yoga, karate, swimming, skiing, skating, kayaking, paddle boarding, surfing, jiu jitsu, other martial arts and other individual sports

3. Reading – The library is full of books and videos on every subject and for every taste imaginable. Ask the librarian to help you choose something you will enjoy, or sign up to join a book club.

4. Hobbies and crafts – Visit a hobby shop and choose a model to build, a sewing or knitting class to sign up for, a kit of some sort to assemble or another similar activity that you find of interest. Be adventurous. Try something new!

5. Take an in-school or after-school class, either online or in person, to explore something you've never done before. Do you want to learn to dance, cook, speak a foreign language, learn art history or take better photos?

6. Visit zoos, aquariums, local historical places, museums, parks, and the beach, or take a walking tour of your town or a city near you.

7. Learn about the natural world by studying up on bees and beekeeping, birds and bird or birdcall identification, gardening and/or volunteering at your local wildlife rehabilitation center or environmental protection/education center.

8. Find a series of podcasts that interest you. There are podcasts on every conceivable topic—finances, music, government, religion, cooking, technology, stories that are pure entertainment, etc.

9. Invite friends over for a get-together or game night. You could have people over for a potluck dinner where everyone brings something. Teach them a board or card game after the meal.

10. Have your own film festival. Line up a series of movies or a TV series and watch them on your own, or invite family or friends to join you. Make popcorn and serve root beer.

11. Go camping with friends or family. Learn to fish.

12. Take art or ceramics lessons.

13. Take music lessons and practice in your free time.

14. Choose a college or professional sports team to follow. Learn the players by name and what is involved in playing their position.

15. Take some singing lessons and then join a choir or other singing group. Do karaoke.

16. Write letters, cards or thank you notes (remember handwritten notes?) to friends and relatives. Put their birthdays on your calendar and send them a greeting.

17. Join a school or community theater group. Act, do lighting, pass out programs, sew costumes, etc.

Your Ideas

Now it's your turn! List five things that you like to do for fun that are possibilities for your free time.

1. _____

2. _____

3. _____

4. _____

5. _____

Pick one that you can do really soon, like this week! _____

_____

_____

Now, after you have done it, write about your experience. What was it like doing this activity? Is it something you'll do again?

_____

_____

_____

_____

It's important that you have things to do in your free time that are fun and give you pleasure. If you do things that you notice trigger your cravings, be sure to note this and speak with your sponsor, therapist or a sober friend about the experience right away. It may be best to avoid that activity for a time until you have been in recovery longer. It is also possible that this activity that triggers your craving is something to just let go of permanently.

This brings us to the topic of renunciation. Big word! The definition of renunciation is "to abandon or sacrifice something." Most often, we renounce something in order to get something we consider to be better. For example, diabetics (hopefully) renounce sugar. You may have to renounce certain activities and maybe even the people associated with them in order to maintain your recovery, which is priceless. This is an important topic, because there will definitely be times when former friends, and even family, will encourage you to participate in something "fun," when you know that, for you, it will lead into dangerous or even deadly territory.

For example, we know a teenager who used to spend hours playing video games, to the point that he would neglect to eat, sleep, or even go to the bathroom. He eventually got some support to change his lifestyle and began to feel much better as he reconnected with the other parts of his life that he had forgotten he enjoyed—like playing sports, hiking, and spending time with friends. But he had one group of friends whose only activity when they got together was to play video games. Whenever he hung out with them, he'd get sucked back into this harmful habit and have to begin the recovery process again. This is often the situation with teens and drinking as well—for example, another teen loved to go dancing with a group of girlfriends, but drinking was always involved with this particular group. Eventually, she had to let those friends go because they weren't interested in going dancing without drinking. Sometimes one seemingly harmless activity leads to a definitely harmful activity. Be aware of this chain reaction and note it. And, remember, your recovery is the best guarantee that your life will be joyful, so don't compromise it for anyone or anything!

List any activities that you know of that trigger your depression, anxiety or craving.

_____

_____

_____

_____

_____

_____

List any friends or family that you are aware of who think it's fun to encourage you to drink, use, self-harm or engage in other activities that are risky for you.

_____

_____

_____

_____

_____

_____

You may think it is odd to be talking about this in a chapter on recreation, but it is often during social, leisure-time activities that you are faced with important decisions regarding activities that are helpful to your recovery and friends who are a positive or negative influence. This is also where the topic of assertiveness comes in, because you need to be assertive in order to avoid people and activities that jeopardize your recovery, and maintain good boundaries.

Write about your ability or lack thereof to assert yourself regarding leisure activities that could trigger cravings. What supports you in saying no?

_____

_____

_____

_____

_____

_____

_____

Talk with your sponsor, therapist or group members about how to manage situations where someone or something triggers a craving in you. Make some notes below about the conversation or your ideas for managing this sort of situation.

_____

_____

_____

_____

_____

Please notice that we did not include engaging in social media, video games or other screen-related activities in this chapter on recreation (except for the suggestion to host a group movie or TV viewing). Research shows that these activities can be addicting and can increase feelings of anxiety, depression and loneliness, rather than alleviate them. Do you spend too much time looking at screens during leisure?

_____

_____

_____

_____

_____

One other recreation topic we have not addressed is sexual pleasure. The reason is that it just seems like too big of a topic for the purposes of this workbook. But it is a topic around which recovering teens may have confusion or difficulty. Speak to your therapist, sponsor or group members about sexual issues and follow their suggestions in this area.

Let's review the potential benefits of recreation as it relates to optimizing mental health and supporting recovery.

The Benefits of Recreation and Leisure Activities

1. Allows for creativity
2. Creates a sense of control and accomplishment
3. Creates a sense of freedom
4. Decreases stress and tension
5. Provides fun and pleasure
6. Gives a sense of personal well-being
7. Supports life balance
8. Provides healthy forms of escape
9. Helps regulate sleeping and eating
10. Leads to self-discovery
11. Reduces boredom
12. Serves as an effective coping strategy
13. Strengthens relationships and encourages bonding
14. Releases "feel-good" chemicals called endorphins, especially when you laugh!

Leisure activities, play and laughter help to take the focus off stress, troubles or whatever is worrying you. The shared experience with other people who are involved in a game or adventure fosters a sense of belonging. If you have been feeling lonely or bored, choose something fun to do, invite a friend/friends and just do it! Be silly! Laugh a lot!

CHAPTER 5

Relationships: We Influence Each Other and We Need Each Other

Treasure your relationships, not your possessions.
—Anthony J. D'Angelo

The Reasons Why

Healthy relationships are an essential element of a fulfilled life. Philosophers, psychologists and scientists, as well as extensive research agree that the quality of our relationships is one of the most important of all lifestyle factors in determining the quality of our lives. They can be an immense force for good or a serious hindrance for recovering teens. Rich relationships lower the risk of disease, ranging from the common cold to heart disease and strokes, and from psychological disorders such as depression.

Social neuroscience shows that we are hardwired for empathy and intimacy. Our brains resonate with one another like tuning forks, picking up subtle emotional and social cues, enabling us to empathize with others. We need one another, plain and simple; it's the human condition. Bonding with others affords us the opportunity to find purpose, feel connected and experience feelings of safety.

These benefits extend to all types of relationships, including close friendships, romantic relationships, and family relationships. While friendships, as well as romantic and sexual connections, are very important in a teenager's life, relationships with family members often have the biggest impact—so prioritizing and nurturing them will have a long-term positive effect on your wellbeing.

When it comes to friendships and partners, it is essential for teens to develop mutually supportive relationships with others who are supportive of your recovery. The person you're with should always support the choices and behaviors that help you reach your recovery goals and enhance your wellbeing.

Noted physician Dr. Dean Ornish has this to say about the importance of relationships to our mental health, "I am not aware of any other factor in medicine—not diet, not smoking, not exercise, not stress, not genetics, not drugs, not surgery—that has greater impact on our quality of life, incidence of illness, and premature death from all causes." Wow! That's quite a statement and a good reason to examine and clean up our relationships.

The list of researchers studying relationships and their importance to physical and mental health is long. There are endless self-help and professional programs for improving our relationship skills, and from all indications, this is an area that is most critical to optimizing resilience and mental health, so we recommend taking advantage of any of the offerings you can find at your school or local community center.

According to Moran Cerf, a neuroscientist at Northwestern University who has been studying decision-making for many years, the surest way to maximize happiness and mental health has nothing to do with experiences, material goods or personal philosophy. It's essentially about whom you choose to spend time with. His neuroscience research has found that when two people are in each other's company, their brain waves will begin to look identical. The more he studied relationships, the more he was able to see that just being next to certain people actually aligns your brain with theirs. In other words, we become more like the people we associate with … and they become more like us. This makes it clear that carefully choosing the people you hang out with is critical to your mental health.

Who are your closest non-using friends? _____

_____

_____

_____

_____

_____

_____

If you feel that your friends will not be open to helping you maintain recovery in this way, please think about how you are valued in these relationships and what is necessary for you to have safety as you navigate recovery. Make some comments here regarding any thoughts you have about this.

_____

_____

_____

_____

_____

_____

Science journalist Daniel Goleman notes that our brain's very design makes it sociable, and inexorably drawn into an intimate brain-to-brain link-up whenever we engage with another person. That neural bridge lets us affect the brain—and so the body—of everyone we interact with, just as they do us. Among people around the world, nourishing relationships are the single most universally agreed-upon feature of a good life.

Name three people you want to **be** more like, who you want to **think** more like, and who **inspire** your recovery. Tell us why you admire them.

1. _____

_____

_____

_____

_____

2. _____

_____

_____

_____

3. _____

_____

_____

_____

_____

_____

Write about the ways in which you believe that being with these three people supports and inspires your recovery just by association.

_____

_____

_____

_____

_____

_____

What do you want in a close friend?

_____

_____

_____

_____

_____

Do you have "sober" friends? "Normie" friends? Please describe here.

_____

_____

_____

_____

_____

The various researchers tell us that good relationships with a variety of family, friends, co-workers and partners improve our cognitive capacity and intelligence, increase our levels of happiness and improve our general physical health and even our longevity.

Unfortunately, social isolation is increasing; it began to increase with the advent of television and has continued with the endless hours we spend on technology. When you have satisfactory relationships, you increase what is called your social capital. With current levels of social capital decreasing, relationships suffer—so now more than ever, you need to think about and cultivate better relationship skills. Make some notes about how many minutes/hours you spend using technology that could be spent in personal relationship.

_____

_____

_____

_____

_____

_____

_____

_____

Researchers, including Dr. Walsh, Dr. Ornish and Drs. John and Julie Gottman, tell us that satisfactory relationships are the number-one, most important positive influence for mental health. But what do they say about how to create them?

If you hope to improve all of your relationships, whether everyday friendships, connections with co-workers or intimate relationships, look to the wisdom of the Gottmans. When it comes to healthy relationships, they are the sages of our time. Their recommendations are based on many years of scientific research in their so-called "Love Lab" at the University of Washington. And although they have focused their work on couples, their advice is generally suitable for most types of relationships. Everything they write about in their various books and articles is practical and can be put to immediate use. For example, one of their recommendations is found in two contrasting words: softness/harshness.

Soft starts and soft endings to our sentences are healthy, strong and healing. They lead to connection, respect and nurture. David Cheek, M.D., says, "Words are magic; they wound or they heal. Take your pick." The Gottmans have proven in their research that this is a fact.

Harsh starts and harsh endings to your sentences are unhealthy, weak and destructive. They typically lead to pain and drama. You must ask yourself, *Is my purpose to heal or wound?* Because your words will be either **neutral**, **healing** or **wounding** … take your pick!

In addition, harsh words typically create drama and drama is ALWAYS an indulgence. So do not indulge yourself and avoid relationships that create or maintain drama.

Name-calling, blaming, accusing, controlling, humiliating the other, being unwilling to see or listen to another person's point of view and pouting, among other negative behaviors, are harsh, and can be relationship killers. They are indicators that you are in need of better relationship skills. Developing those skills is part of the work of maturing into an adult.

When we use harsh words or behave aggressively, the other person will feel attacked and respond defensively. There is no hope of healing with this approach, and no helpful communication will occur.

A soft approach does not accuse or blame anyone; rather, it is an invitation to a conversation. It allows each person to take responsibility for themselves. If the person you are talking to becomes defensive, or if you become defensive, it means that one or both of you are not really listening to or understanding the other. Take a deep breath and try to listen for understanding, in which case, there is no need to be defensive.

Write a little about the person in your life who has taught you the most about managing a kind, respectful relationship.

_____

_____

_____

_____

_____

_____

Maintaining appropriate boundaries is essential to healthy relationships. Boundaries define what is and is not acceptable to you in your relationships.

There are many types of relationships, such as kinship, social, business, activity, collegial, transactional, intimate and romantic. How you communicate, what information you share about yourself, who you spend time with and how you give of yourself depends upon your personal goals and how you want to live your life. When your boundaries are weak, unguarded or unclear, you let in all sorts of people and experiences that aren't healthy. So, be discerning and have appropriate boundaries in your various relationships.

Clarity is the friend of healthy relationship. So, be crystal clear about your particular boundaries in relationships. For example, what are your boundaries about borrowing and lending money? What are your sexual boundaries? What are your boundaries about being on time or lateness? This list is endless and essential. Think about your physical, sexual, verbal, financial and material boundaries, as well as any other categories you can think of that define your boundaries. This will take some time and effort, and it will be important to discern the boundaries of others to whom you relate. Remember, there are not necessarily right or wrong answers to these questions. Your boundaries are yours. When you know what they are, you can more easily negotiate relationships with others who may agree or disagree with you.

Use these pages to write about the various types of boundaries mentioned above and your thoughts about each.

_____

_____

_____

_____

_____

_____

_____

_____

_____

_____

_____

_____

_____

_____

_____

_____

_____

_____

_____

_____

_____

_____

_____

_____

_____

_____

_____

_____

_____

_____

_____

_____

Reciprocity is generally part of healthy relationships. It means that we do for each other; the friendship or relationship is not a one-way street with one person doing all the giving or getting. There is no need to keep score on who did what when. You can generally feel that the relationship is equally give and take. Write about your understanding of reciprocity in your relationships. Are you a giver? A taker? Or, is it mostly pretty even?

_____

_____

_____

_____

_____

_____

_____

Because it is true that we become more like the company we keep, it is important that you choose people to hang out with who are more skilled in healthy relationship than you are. You will learn by observation, and they can be a source of information and inspiration when you have questions about things like how to manage a disagreement with a friend, relative or partner; how to have better family relationships; how to be a better parent, etc. Who can you identify who can teach you about healthy relationships at home, in the workplace or at school and in the community? For example, if you want to learn more about good romantic relationships, talk to people who have had long, satisfying marriages. If you want to have better work relationships, talk to someone who manages work well, etc. Sometimes people hold themselves up as experts in these areas, but have been unable to accomplish the very thing they are supposedly expert at. Look for teachers and mentors who have actually accomplished what they claim to teach.

Write about who might help you learn more about relationships and boundaries in these various areas we have identified, and any others you can think of. If you're not sure, how will you find these helpers? If you need more space, use the pages at the end of the workbook.

_____

_____

_____

_____

_____

_____

Almost always, recovery means that relationships will change and some will go by the wayside. "Friends" who were toxic or only interested in partying must be relinquished. This can be a relief, or it can be very painful. Let's hope that somewhere down the line they will catch the recovery train, too, and you can have a friendship in recovery. Until then, let them go. Really! Let them go! Make a list of the people that you must let go of and make note of how you feel about it.

_____
_____
_____
_____
_____
_____
_____

Always remember: Violence, whether verbal, emotional, physical or sexual, has no place in a healthy relationship and is a threat to mental health and recovery. If you are experiencing violence in a relationship, seek help immediately from someone you trust. Do not ever assume that your aggressor can change by themselves, or with your help. Impossible! They will need professional help to change.

Are there aggressors who you should avoid? Write about that here.

_____
_____
_____
_____
_____
_____
_____
_____
_____
_____
_____

Some of your self-discovery work may be very scary as you confront some unfortunate past behaviors, experiences and pain. With diligent work, you can accept who you once were, and who you are today. Hopefully, you will eventually find forgiveness for yourself for past behavior and hold yourself accountable to a newly developed set of healthy boundaries and relationship skills. Self-awareness is key in healthy relationship. Being able to see your own part in challenging situations and correcting it to the best of your ability makes room for possible repair.

Learning how to select and nurture relationships is a skill in and of itself. This is critically important.

Possible Actions for Implementation

- Read books on boundaries and practice communicating them
- Enroll in a class for teens on improving your communication skills
- Read self-help books about relationships
- Practice "soft starts" during challenging communication
- Learn about others by asking questions about them
- Make a new friend who is somewhat different from you (a different race, religion, socio-economic level, profession, etc.)
- Make a habit of remembering people's birthdays and other important events in their lives
- Be a good friend to yourself, taking good care of yourself

Your Ideas

Write a bit about what you know about your relationship patterns that have to do with YOU. Start by noting the repeating patterns of relationship in your life, as you are able to identify them.

_____

_____

_____

_____

What are the things you do in relationships that seem to work well?

What are the things you do in relationships that do not work well and are in need of change?

Acknowledging your past honestly will help you stop doing things that cause damage, hurt or pain to yourself and others and begin a better life. When you do your fourth Step in a 12-Step program, you will be able to better identify your own behaviors that have harmed your relationships. People often approach a fourth Step with trepidation, but with the firm but loving guidance of your sponsor, you will find valuable information and relief. It will give you an opportunity to identify some of your relationship-killing behaviors and the possibility of making changes, as you choose.

Have you done a fourth Step? If not, are you concerned about it? If you have completed a fourth Step, what did you learn about your relationship patterns?

_____

_____

_____

_____

_____

_____

If you are not in a 12-Step program, you can still take an inventory of your relationships and determine your part in harming them or being harmed by them. It is important to learn from your past behavior that has been destructive, and also to learn who in your life supports your recovery and who detracts from it.

There's another type of relationship that provides valuable benefits: a relationship with a pet. Pets offer unconditional love and help you learn about yourself, build relationships with other people and learn responsibility. While you may have lost some friends as you made changes in your life, a pet is loyal and will respond to affection. Having the responsibility for another living creature is a fantastic way to encourage discipline and responsibility on a daily basis. No matter what kind of animal you choose, pets can be a great comfort as well as a fun and loving companion on your healing journey. Consider talking with your family about adding a pet—or another pet—to the household.

Do you have a pet? If so, please describe.

_____

_____

_____

_____

_____

_____

Benefits of Healthy Relationships

- Learn, mature and see new possibilities
- Strengthen emotional and social interactions with others
- Share ideas, advice, experiences in confidence
- Support and help each other heal
- Share love and caring
- Assist in reducing conflicts and meeting challenges
- Provide a buffer against stress
- Be healthier and live longer
- Experience more life satisfaction

Good friends can be good medicine. Since this TLC has been identified as the most important of all eight, be sure to spend sufficient time and effort to sort out this area of your life. Understand that good relationships require time, effort and reciprocity. Choose wisely, as you become like the company you keep. It will be well worth it!

CHAPTER 6

Time in Nature: A Source of Healing

Nature is God's reset button for our minds, bodies, and spirits.
—Michael Hyatt

The Reasons Why

Time in nature, though proven to be a great healing force, has become a luxury for many of us living in the Western industrialized world. Think of it! Unlike our grandparents and ancestors farther back, we are living mostly indoors under artificial lighting, in manufactured environments. In 1900, only 15% of the world's population lived in urban areas. The remaining 85% lived in rural areas, where nature was everywhere around. By some estimates, by 2050, over 70% of the world's population will live in urban settings, removed from much of the naturally occurring world.

Some psychologists and educators have called this state of affairs Nature Deficit Disorder. They say that modern people, by cutting themselves off from nature, have cut themselves off from the nature of their own being, because we humans are a part of nature, too, and dependent on it.

Whether we're in our homes, cars, schools or workplaces, we spend most of our days removed from nature—and it's proving not to be good for us. Research consistently supports the connection between time in nature and improved psychological health: Stress, anxiety, anger and gloom diminish, and optimism, self-esteem and vitality increase. By contrast, walking through a shopping mall has been shown to raise stress and lower self-esteem. This shouldn't be surprising given our million years or so of evolution out in the natural world. Since the 1980s, we have spent 90–95% of our time indoors—a first in human history.

Many people relate to the notion that a particular aspect of the natural world is "my special place," or a place that helped shape them. It might be the mountains, the forests, the waterways, the open spaces of meadows or grasslands, the desert or some other place. In the space below, write about this special place and its meaning for you. If you haven't identified your favorite place in nature, think about a pleasant memory that took place outdoors and write about that.

_____

_____

_____

_____

_____

_____

Nowadays, how often are you able to spend time in this particular place, or somewhere similar?

_____

_____

There are many psychological, physical and spiritual benefits to connecting with the natural world. Recovering people in particular, and people in general, find that regular contact with nature is beneficial. Time spent outdoors leads to relief from stress, increased attention and awareness, experiences of trust and reduced need for control, and is one of the most common triggers for peak spiritual experiences. That's why Adventure Therapy is one of the modalities we utilize at Newport Academy—the experience of being immersed in a physical activity while surrounded by the beauty of nature is profoundly healing.

Emotional numbing is one possible result of nature deficit; it means that you have no emotional response to something that would ordinarily cause you to have a feeling of some sort. If you are not outdoors, then you have no experience of the joy and awe of seeing aspects of the beauty of nature. Buzzing bees, the intricacies of flowers, the majesty of trees, and the crash of ocean waves are all there to delight your senses, if only you are outdoors to witness them.

Likewise, you may have no sadness or anger at the pollution that is in the oceans and waterways, the trash by the side of the road and the destruction of the habitats of our animal friends. Their suffering is far removed from you if you are never outdoors to witness to it.

Do you see any symptoms of emotional numbing in yourself? Please write about that here.

_____

_____

_____

_____

_____

_____

_____

_____

_____

_____

_____

Our always **on**, never-disconnected way of living robs us of the rejuvenation provided by regularly experiencing the natural world. Though amazing technological advances have enabled us to live in urban environments and lightened the loads of physical labor, it has been at a considerable physical and psychological cost, as we have distanced from the natural world that sustains us. This disconnection affects us in multiple ways and has ultimately led to the degradation of the earth that is threatening our very survival. This is an important aspect of spending time in nature, because typically, the more we notice the natural world around us—the birds, the trees and plants, the squirrels, deer, raccoons and other woodland creatures—the more we tend to care about the preservation of nature in all its forms, which is also about our own survival.

Write about the aspects of nature that you most enjoy and how you feel when you see, hear, smell or otherwise experience them.

_____

_____

_____

_____

_____

_____

Living in the world of media—a world of images and dialogue, which can be interesting and expansive—comes at the cost of your own personal experience out in the world. The natural world is the real world.

How much time do you spend on media (television, computer, phone, etc.) compared to being outdoors? Give the ratio if you can.

_____

_____

_____

_____

_____

_____

How nature deficient are you? Do you have Nature Deficit Disorder? Reconnecting with the great outdoors can help lift depression, improve energy and boost overall feelings of wellbeing and mental health. Being in nature has long been associated with being mindful and meditative, but only recently has the scientific community researched the mental health benefits of outdoor immersion. It delivers not only health benefits, but also wider social benefits and cost savings that medication does not. Active, social and adventurous contact with nature may be combined with other interventions to protect and enhance your health and wellbeing, as well as contributing to the treatment of chronic mental, emotional and physical health difficulties. Although an hour a day is better, even spending just 20 minutes outside per day can boost your energy levels and produce a greater sense of vitality.

Realistically, how much time do you believe you can spend outdoors on a regular basis? During the week? On the weekend?

_____

_____

_____

_____

_____

_____

Consciously incorporating a natural environmental component into your integrated therapeutic lifestyle changes makes sense for teens in recovery. The benefits of nature for body, mind and soul are finding their way to prescription pads, too, as more healthcare providers are telling their patients to take a hike—literally. Doctors and therapists give their patients "nature prescriptions" to help treat a variety of medical conditions, from alcoholism and drug abuse to post-cancer fatigue, obesity, high blood pressure, diabetes and mental health disorders.

Two so-called eco-therapies that are often used in inpatient and outpatient treatment settings that reconnect you with the rest of nature are animal-assisted therapy and horticultural therapy. There is no doubt that creating relationships of trust, kindness and playfulness with animals is a healing experience. Likewise, creating beauty in nature through gardening, whether for food or flowers, requires patience, responsibility and following directions. These have increasingly been proven to be effective ways of relieving the loneliness and disconnection experienced by many people, and especially those who have suffered from mental health conditions. In the space below, please write about either or both of these two interventions, time with animals and/or time gardening, and how it might be possible to incorporate one of these into your overall program of recovery. Don't forget that gardening can take place with potted plants if you don't have a yard to work in, and that working with indoor plants counts, too.

In this space, write about your favorite experience with an animal:

_____

_____

_____

_____

_____

_____

In this space, write about your best experience growing something for food or beauty:

_____

_____

_____

_____

_____

_____

_____

How can nature help you avoid relapse and have a healthier life? Years of research have confirmed evidence that eco or green therapy has regenerative powers, improving mood and easing anxiety, stress and depression. Reconnection with the natural world is a freely available activity that can help you heal and thrive. Being in nature, or even viewing scenes of nature, reduces anger, fear and stress, and increases pleasant feelings. Exposure to nature contributes to your physical wellbeing, reducing blood pressure, heart rate, muscle tension and the production of stress hormones. In addition, nature helps us cope with pain. The health effects of green space are wide-ranging, and show strong associations between access to nature and longer, healthier lives.

Researchers at the University of Illinois discovered that green outdoor spaces relieve the symptoms of Attention Deficit Disorder (ADD)—the greener the setting, the more the relief. By contrast, indoor activities, such as watching television or playing on paved, non-green areas, increase the symptoms of ADD. In a similar vein, MacArthur Genius Award recipient Majora Carter, in her work called *Greening the Ghetto*, found research indicating that where there are trees and vegetation in neighborhoods, crime is reduced. She started planting trees and building bike paths and parks in her neighborhood in New York City to support the health and wellbeing of the community. Clearly, time in nature has a significant impact on our moods and behavior if it can even reduce the crime rate.

In the space below, name several places within easy walking distance of your treatment center, home and workplace where you can spend time in nature.

_____

_____

_____

_____

_____

_____

A chapter on time in nature would not be complete without mentioning Vitamin D as an important nutrient for healing. Getting enough of this vitamin (which may actually be a hormone) is critical for maintaining a healthy immune system, and sunlight is the means of getting it. Vitamin D forms right on your skin when you are outdoors. Though you can take Vitamin D supplements, its best to get it from natural sources, meaning the sun! By helping maximize calcium absorption, Vitamin D promotes bone and dental health. It can also elevate mood and reduce the risk of cancer, heart disease, Alzheimer's, stroke, diabetes and more. Vitamin D also improves blood flow and lowers blood pressure by literally relaxing your blood vessels. While we all know to protect ourselves from the sun to avoid skin cancer, we also need Vitamin D for bone growth, cell growth, inflammation reduction and neuromuscular and immune function. "Sensible sun exposure" means only going out in the sun for about one-third to one-half the amount of time it would take your skin to mildly burn, or roughly 10 to 15 minutes for many. After you've gotten a bit of Vitamin D, reach for the sunscreen and continue your exploration of the great outdoors.

Spending too much time inside, away from natural light and with increased exposure to artificial light, can alter your circadian rhythms, thus disrupting your sleep pattern. Your internal body clock is naturally tied to the sun's schedule. Early-morning exposure to sunlight has been shown to help recalibrate these sleep cycles. A few consecutive days outside on a camping or backpacking trip will get the job done much faster. Natural light normalizes your sleep schedule by assisting in the regulation of the melatonin system, and sound, uninterrupted sleep is essential to recovery. Difficulty sleeping is a big component of substance abuse and other mental health problems.

Write about your quality of sleep. Do you wake up rested? Do you need more outdoor time to ease any sleep problems?

_____

_____

_____

_____

_____

Your body has to work hard to get the oxygen it needs to function in polluted or indoor environments. This raises your heart rate and blood pressure. As you learned in the chapter on relaxation, breathing techniques have the ability to dampen the production of stress hormones as well as train your body's reaction to stressful situations. Rapid breathing engages your body's sympathetic nervous system (your "fight or flight, freeze" response), which is activated by stress and works to energize the body. Slow, deep breathing—the kind encouraged by the great outdoors—stimulates the body's parasympathetic reaction, which calms us down. Whether you are running on a fitness trail or just looking at trees at a playground, you can reduce your blood pressure as well as the stress-related hormones cortisol and adrenaline.

"Forest bathing," so named by the Japanese, involves trips into the woods for 90 minutes or more that can significantly decrease your anxiety, depression, anger, confusion and fatigue. And because stress inhibits the immune system, the stress-reduction benefits of being among the trees are further magnified. But, remember, even just five minutes in a garden, park, or by the water may improve your short-term working memory and overall health.

Spending time in nature has been linked to improved attention spans (short and long term), boosts in serotonin (the feel-good neurotransmitter) and increased activity in the parts of the brain responsible for empathy, emotional stability and love (whereas urban environments do the same for fear and anxiety). If you're feeling down, get outside.

Teenagers' lives are busier than ever with jobs, school, sports, socializing and family life. Trying to focus on many activities or even a single thing for long periods of time can mentally drain you, a phenomenon called "Directed Attention Fatigue." Spending time in the outdoors, looking at plants, water, birds, mountains and other aspects of nature gives the cognitive, thinking portion of the brain a break, allowing you to focus better and renew your ability to be present and patient. Whether you are hiking, gardening, birding, building sand castles or simply sitting and observing, nature provides opportunities to relax, refresh and improve focus and concentration.

Elements of the environment, such as the smell of the wood, the sound of a running stream of water, and the vibrant colors of the forest can provide relaxation and reduce stress, which may lower your levels of cortisol, pulse rate, and blood pressure. Physicians and psychologists have long known that sunlight is a good treatment for seasonal affective disorder (SAD). There's a world of benefit to being out in nature.

Do you have a natural setting you can retreat to when you feel stressed? Where do you go and what do you like about it?

_____

_____

_____

_____

_____

What natural items (for example, plants, animals, shells, rocks, feathers, artwork) have you brought indoors into your living space to remind you of the natural world?

_____

_____

_____

_____

_____

What you focus your mind on when you are outdoors is important. Clear your mind of any thoughts other than what you are seeing and experiencing. Focus on the sights, sounds and smells around you to relax your mind. You'll return from your time in nature refreshed and ready for other activities of the day.

Possible Actions for Implementation

Find your own meaning in the natural world and the adventures you experience there. Here are some activities you can start incorporating into your everyday life, as well as some possible assignments for time in nature:

1. Take a 20-minute walk outdoors every day. During your walk, focus on the various aspects of nature that you encounter and keep a journal of what you observe. How many birds or other critters did you see? How many trees did you pass and what kind were they? Did you see flowers? If so, what colors and kinds did you see? The point is to be truly present for your time in nature in a way that allows you to appreciate the experience.

2. Walk your dog or offer to walk someone else's dog on a new route from time to time and observe new surroundings. It's nice to have a companion on your outdoor adventures.

3. Sit outdoors and simply observe for 20 minutes. Notice what you see, what you smell, what you feel (the sun or rain on your face) and what you hear during that time and remember the moment and/or write about it.

4. If you live near the ocean where there are tide pools, take a magnifying glass to them and see what you can see.

5. Find a tree that you like and observe the patterns of the bark. Be able to describe it in your journal, i.e., color, texture, pattern, smell. What does it feel like to hug a tree? Go ahead! Do it!

6. Spend time gardening. If it is winter or you don't live where this is a possibility, bring nature inside by planting a windowsill herb garden, or tend other indoor plants.

7. Combine time in nature with other areas of *8 Ways,* such as exercising outdoors, climbing hills, playing outdoor sports with friends, taking a nap outdoors at the beach, flying a kite, picnicking in the woods with your family or volunteering in local clean-up activities.

8. Choose one aspect of nature to focus on. Let's say you have decided to observe an ant colony today. As you observe the ants at work, ask yourself what they can teach you about recovery and life in general. What is the metaphor for your own life that is in progress as you observe? Write your observations in your journal. Taking lessons from nature is a powerful exercise!

9. Find an outdoor labyrinth and walk it.

10. If you want to feel the energy of earth, lie down on the grass or sand, or go barefoot at the beach or park. The earth has a magnetic field, and you can feel it if you are still enough and there is quiet. Bringing your body into the same frequency as that magnetic field is called "grounding." Grounding can have an intense anti-inflammatory and energizing effect on the body. Nature's calming effect comes from not only the fresh air, but also the ground.

Your Ideas

We've given you some ideas for your time in nature. In the space below, write a few more possibilities that reflect things you could do that would be enjoyable to you and that you are likely to actually do. Be a little adventurous! Try to add activities in nature that enrich your everyday experience of life and reignite whatever interest you have had in the natural world, of which you are an integral part! Try to get at least five more suggestions to add to ours.

1. _____

2. _____

3. _____

4. _____

5. _____

Use this chart to schedule time in nature each day for the next seven days, along with documenting your experience. There are more pages for you to extend this chart in the Appendix.

Nature Activity	Location	Time Spent	Feelings/Sensations/ Mood Before	Feelings/Sensations/ Mood After

Benefits of Time in Nature

- Accelerates recovery from surgery or illness
- Alleviates mental fatigue
- Boosts fitness if combined with exercise
- Boosts self-confidence
- Boosts immune function
- Clears the mind
- Enhances cognitive function
- Enlivens your senses
- Fuels imagination
- Improves mood
- Improves sleep
- Increases the ability to focus, even in children
- Increases energy level
- Increases your awareness
- Lowers blood pressure
- Reduces stress
- Reduces symptoms of depression

When we spend more time in nature, we are more willing to participate in its preservation. Environmental concerns are at critical proportions. When you are aware of your natural environment, you will become more conscious of your own impact and hopefully become a better steward of this beautiful outdoors that has been gifted to us.

CHAPTER 7

Giving Back: Giving the Gift of Generosity

We make a living by what we get, but we make a life by what we give.
—Winston Churchill

The Reasons Why

Giving from our abundance is a proven way to increase our feelings of self-worth and self-confidence. So often, mental health challenges rob us of any feeling of generosity or a balanced and regular practice of giving. This does not mean that you are inherently selfish. It means that in the throes of anxiety, depression, trauma, or addiction, you are in a state of consciousness in which it is difficult to access the more altruistic parts of yourself. Some recovering people cannot imagine that they have anything worth giving, or that anyone would want what they have to offer.

Part of the antidote to mental health and substance abuse issues is to reverse the feeling of "never enough." People who are suffering generally do not have the mental energy to think about altruism, or the physical energy to devote to it.

Most people have a desire to be helpful to others. Not only does it feel good to uplift others or contribute to the community in some way, it adds to a sense of meaning and shifts our energy from loneliness and separation to joy and connection.

12-Step programs emphasize "getting a commitment," which typically means volunteering for one of any number of tasks before, during and after meetings, such as being a greeter, setting up chairs, making coffee, arranging a literature table or cleaning up afterwards. Sponsors usually make getting a commitment a recommendation or requirement early on in their sponsoring of a newcomer. There is wisdom behind this suggestion, as research supports giving back as a powerful way to wellbeing.

Dr. Roger Walsh, in his book *Essential Spirituality*, suggests that when beginning to nurture a nature of generosity, it is important to start small. He recommends looking for small ways of giving to others with no expectation of getting anything in return. It is often a habit of recovering people to overdo, perhaps from guilt, or trying to make up for lost time or simply not having much experience with estimating time and energy allotments for these new practices. Dr. Walsh quotes Mother Teresa, who urged, "Don't look for spectacular actions. What is important is the gift of yourself. It is the degree of love you insert in your deeds." So, starting small is good advice, and remembering to add the love is essential.

In addition, Dr. Walsh advises finding ways to give that you enjoy. If you find volunteer activities and opportunities that you enjoy, you are more likely to continue doing them. Sometimes this requires experimentation because you may not know what sort of volunteering will be enjoyable. Be adventurous and try some different volunteer activities and see what fits. You might like volunteering to bathe dogs at your local Humane Society, or playing with the animals there so that they remain socialized and more likely to be adopted. People in nursing homes enjoy visitors, and maybe your local library has a literacy program where you can volunteer to teach an adult to read or re-shelve books. Community organizations of all sorts are always looking for volunteers for a variety of tasks. At the same time, small acts, such as phoning a relative who hasn't heard from you in a while, just to say hi, definitely count, as does holding the door for someone, walking their dog or offering to babysit for an hour or two while your friend grocery shops. Do what you can, and make it a habit.

Giving back is a proven means to good health and happiness. The practice of gratitude through giving back can be transformational in supporting recovery, re-entering the world as a person in recovery, and sustaining long-term wellness. In a recent speech, Dr. Joycelyn Elders, our former U.S. Surgeon General, said, "When the ladder has been lowered down so that you can climb up, be sure to lower that ladder again, so that the next person can climb up, too." Certainly, the twelfth Step of 12-Step programs supports this value, when it states, "Having had a spiritual awakening as the result of following these steps, we tried to carry this message to alcoholics..." The idea, of course, is to give back or "pay forward" what has so generously been given to you.

We believe that many of the maladies of today's society have to do with a general lack of meaning to our lives and a self-centered focus. Turning your gaze outside yourself, and beginning to contribute to the world's work, can start a process of expanded awareness of the world around you, and the ways in which you can make a difference in that world. Certainly this mindset has the potential to improve your relationships with others and increase your own self-esteem. President John F. Kennedy, in his famous speech, said, "Ask not what your country can do for you. Ask what you can do for your country." Well, we are suggesting the same thing, but expanding on that thought to suggest that when you offer up your help and support of others, whether human, animal or the natural environment, you are doing something that improves your own functioning, too. The exciting thing about this concept is that as you contribute to the world's work, you can experience the joy of service as you develop your character and your leadership skills in a positive way. It is a worthwhile inquiry to consider the ways in which you are meant to be of service in this world. Tommy Rosen, a well-known yoga teacher and advocate of service in recovery, says, "Once you find your means of service, the keys to the kingdom are in your hands."

In the space below, list three ideas you have for giving back or volunteering in your home, place of worship, community or elsewhere.

_____

_____

_____

_____

_____

_____

Giving back helps the giver by reducing painful, unhealthy emotional states such as greed, jealousy and self-centeredness, while strengthening pleasant, healthy emotional states such as happiness, joy and generosity. This is very important because it is common for recovering teens to experience significant depression and/or anxiety as part of what are known as post-acute withdrawal symptoms. Other symptoms, such as restlessness, mood swings, irritability, fatigue, variable energy, disturbed sleep, low enthusiasm and variable concentration, can be part of this picture. Post-acute withdrawal can last a very long time, even months or years. While we know that exercise, good nutrition and the rest of the healthy habits of therapeutic lifestyle choices are important, accessing the mood-altering effects of doing something for someone else is one means of addressing the challenges of recovery and ultimately leads to a more meaningful life.

In the space below, list any symptoms of post-acute withdrawal that you experience.

_____

_____

_____

_____

_____

_____

There is a certain self-discipline that comes from giving back, and self-discipline is important for recovering people. Giving back means that you are using some of your precious time and resources to do something for someone else. It means that you must give up or let go of that time, money or whatever you're giving, as a service for the betterment of another. So, you are going to make a sacrifice of your time, what is convenient or expedient for you, and possibly, your resources. In this process, you will learn to be more focused on the good of the larger community, as opposed to, "what I want right now." You will also need to plan your daily or weekly schedule in a way that allows for your area of service.

Children's Defense Fund founder Marian Wright Edelman says, "Service is the rent we pay for the life we have been given." If you have been given the gift of recovery, never mind the great gift of life itself, then your service is certainly your repayment. Since you live every day in the company of others and the larger society, it is important to do your part to create an atmosphere of kindness and generosity. Generosity usually leads to more generosity. Those of you who participate in acts of kindness and caring behavior are creating a kinder and more caring atmosphere in which to live and work.

Contributions and service to others can produce a potent euphoria, or "helper's high." The neural "glow" from paying it forward even shows up on MRI scans of the brain. We experience this feel-good sensation at a cellular level that boosts everything from our psychological outlook to heart health and immune system. Altruism benefits both physical and mental health, and can even extend the lifespan.

In the space below, list the last act of service that you performed and what you experienced as a result.

_____

_____

_____

Possible Actions for Implementation

There are hundreds of ways of displaying goodwill and generosity. Even the smallest gesture can improve someone else's day as well as your own. What follows is a list of just a very few possibilities for giving back:

- Play an instrument and/or sing at a senior citizen center
- Volunteer in a classroom or for a Scout troop
- Teach someone to read and write through the local library literacy program
- Wash dogs at your local Humane Society
- Send a greeting card to a friend or relative
- Pick up litter and deposit it in a trash can
- Drive a cancer patient to treatment
- Serve on a phone bank for your political party
- Read to a child
- Volunteer at a 12-Step meeting
- Work in a community garden
- Organize a walking group of two or more friends
- Donate clothing, music, books and items you don't use
- Collect canned goods for the local food pantry
- Ride, walk or run for a cause
- Start a lending library or book club
- Visit patients in a VA or nursing home

- Volunteer with Students Against Drunk Driving
- Play sports with kids with special needs
- Open the door for someone
- Contact Volunteers of America (VOA) to find a placement in your area of interest
- Smile at others and offer a compliment while looking them in the eye
- Volunteer in your place of worship
- Write a personal note of gratitude to someone
- Offer to babysit for a friend's children
- Give food coupons to a homeless person
- Treat a friend or relative to coffee, a meal or a movie
- Call your mother or other relative and ask how they are doing
- Offer to take someone's dog for a walk
- Make muffins for your neighbor—whether you know them or not

Moderation and reality are key elements in making health-enhancing decisions. Manage your expectations. You can't do everything, and not everyone will be grateful for what you do. If you begin to feel resistance or resentment, step back and ask yourself if you are doing too much or expecting praise for your generosity. If so, check your motives!

His Holiness the 14th Dalai Lama instructs that we meditate on why we are choosing to do a particular activity. If the answer emerges that you had been told you ought to do it, or should do it, that would be a wrong reason. He advises to do it because you believe it is the right thing to do. Of course, this doesn't mean that you don't take advice from others. But you need to examine the advice, and consider whether it seems like the right thing to do.

Giving to others does not mean distracting yourself from your goals or depleting your energy. Helping others is not a substitute or excuse for not helping yourself. Don't take on too much, too fast. Start slow. Fulfilling your commitments is important, as others will rely on you to do what you said you would do. Keep in mind that following through on things is a healthy habit. By incorporating these eight healthy lifestyle choices into your daily living, you are following through on your promise to yourself and significant others that you will value your recovery, and become and remain trustworthy and truthful. So, don't over-promise and under-deliver. You can always increase your involvement once you know what you can do without needlessly stressing yourself or neglecting your recovery plan. Take on one thing at a time and give it your best.

Ways I currently help others: Frequency (daily, monthly, etc.)

1. _____   _____

2. _____   _____

3. _____   _____

4. _____   _____

5. _____   _____

I help/don't help others because: _____

_____

_____

_____

_____

_____

_____

_____

_____

_____

_____

_____

Your Ideas

List five things you can do this week to give back. There are more pages for you to write on at the end of this workbook.

Helping Act	For Whom	Where	When	How I Felt After

Benefits of Giving Back

- Strengthens your recovery and grounds you in recovery principles
- Gives meaning/purpose to your life
- Helps you discover and enhance your strengths
- Prevents isolation
- Keeps you active
- Helps cultivate gratitude
- Helps to work through guilt, regret and other negative emotions

- Increases self-esteem
- Stimulates the development of new career and social skills
- Builds confidence in your abilities
- Ignites new passions
- Extends life
- Increases happiness
- Expands circle of friends and acquaintances
- Releases natural feel-good chemicals in the brain (endorphins, serotonin, dopamine and oxytocin)

You have received the great gift of life! Use your gift to enhance the lives of others and the world around you.

CHAPTER 8

Spirituality: We Find Our Spiritual Path

We are not humans on a spiritual path. Rather, we are spirits on a human path.
—Jean Shinoda Bolen, M.D.

The Reasons Why

The second Step in all 12-Step programs says, "We came to believe that a power greater than ourselves could restore us to sanity." The third Step says, "We made a decision to turn our will and our lives over to the care of God as we understood Him."

Whether you follow a 12-Step program of recovery or not, a spiritual life is shown by Dr. Walsh's research to be a cornerstone of the *8 Ways to Wellbeing* and the foundation of a healthy life.

Religion and spirituality are vitally important to most people in the world. Some 90% of the world's population engages in religious and spiritual practices. Religious and spiritual beliefs cam be an important part of dealing with life's joys and hardships. Faith communities at their best can provide a sense of purpose and guidelines for living a moral life and character development. Among recovering teens who have been introduced to a 12-Step program, it is the second and third Steps that begin the process of developing a spiritual practice, which will hopefully evolve, grow and deepen as time and recovery continue.

In most healing traditions, and in early Western medicine, concerns of the body and spirit were intertwined. Over time, with the scientific revolution and growth of a medical model and pharmacology, these considerations were ignored or diminished. Today, however, a growing number of studies reveal that spirituality may play a bigger role in the recovery process than previously acknowledged by physicians and scientists. We've learned that the body, mind and spirit are connected and cannot really be separated—each influences the other. The health of any one of these elements seems to affect the others.

Spirituality includes a belief in a power operating in the universe that is greater than oneself, a sense of interconnectedness with all living creatures, an awareness of the purpose and meaning of life and the development of personal values. It's the way we find meaning, cope, are comforted and develop inner peace and reverence for life in all its forms.

There is abundant evidence that the potential for religious or spiritual experience resides in everyone. Spirituality is part of your birthright! How you access and practice this is up to you and must fit with your values and belief system.

Spirituality has enormous healing potential. What seems to be helpful is an inner personal commitment to faith/spirituality and/or religious practice.

Medical studies indicate that spiritual people are less prone to self-destructive behaviors and have less stress, less depression, less physical disability and greater total life satisfaction. Spirituality can reduce depression, improve blood pressure, decrease muscle tension, lower respiratory and heart rates and boost the immune system. People in recovery find that their religious beliefs and/or spiritual practices can help them fight feelings of helplessness, restore meaning and order to life situations and help them regain a sense of control. High levels of hope and optimism—key factors in fighting depression and controlling urges—have been found among those who regularly practice their faith.

Obviously, the benefits of spiritual practice span an array of health measures. People call on their religion or spiritual concepts for help and support when faced with illness as well as emotional and physical stress. Increased resilience and better relationships are also attributed to regular religious and/or spiritual involvement.

The most amazing result seems to be regarding lifespan. Strikingly, Dr. Walsh's research showed that people who attend religious services weekly tend to live seven years longer than those who don't, even when baseline health and behaviors have been statistically controlled.

Noted psychologist and author Charlotte Kasl, Ph.D., wrote an expanded version of several of the 12 Steps, which we offer here. For Step 2, she wrote, "We come to believe that God/ The Goddess/Universe/Great Spirit/Higher Power awakens the healing wisdom within us when we open ourselves to that power." She says that this step, "affirms that a sacred spirit or life force energy is within us and around us. We tap into the power of the universe, draw it in and use it to awaken our inner capacity for healing. We are not separated, isolated beings, we are part of One Energy, connected to the vast universe. Thus it is important that we develop our capacity to be touched by nature and beauty. We learn to see the wonder in small things—from a new leaf to a child's smile."

Say something here about your own understanding of Higher Power.

_____

_____

_____

_____

_____

_____

_____

_____

_____

_____

_____

_____

_____

_____

_____

Now write your own version of Step 2.

_____

_____

_____

_____

_____

_____

_____

_____

_____

_____

_____

Dr. Kasl goes on to offer as part of an expansion of the third Step, "We make a decision to find our authentic selves and trust in the healing power of the truth. Instead of adopting society's inauthentic stereotypes, this step encourages us to reach deep and ask ourselves: Who am I? What do I feel? What is my experience? What feels right for me? What are my dreams, and strengths? Experiencing the healing power of the truth is about minute-to-minute honesty with oneself and others. It's about what you wear, what you eat, and being able to say, Yes, No and Maybe, without justifying yourself or undue worry about what the other person will think or say. It's about being *true* to oneself without guilt. It also affirms that human relations, intimacy and power are grounded in hearing and speaking our truths, simply, kindly and without apology. Ultimately being close to the bones of truth is what creates intimacy, trust, feelings of connection and a quiet mind. This is truly integral to a spiritual way of life."

What things in your life give you a sense of inner peace, comfort, strength, love and connection? This is part of the truth of who you are. Please write about it here.

_____

_____

_____

_____

_____

Who are the people that you get caught up in worrying about in terms of what they think of you? Who do you worry about pleasing?

_____

_____

_____

_____

_____

_____

Spiritual wellness is a personal matter involving values and beliefs that provide a purpose in your life. While different individuals may have different views of what spirituality is, it is generally considered to be the search for meaning and purpose in human existence, leading one to strive for a state of harmony with oneself and others while working to balance inner needs with the rest of the world. For most people, religion and spirituality are especially important in coping with stress and illness, and are beneficial to those in recovery. Authentic spirituality holds us together in our darkest moments, days or weeks. It is anything that leads us toward, contributes to or maintains our health. It gives us the strength and confidence to admit our mistakes, focus on our strengths and offer mercy and forgiveness to ourselves and others.

So, let's talk for a minute about the difference between spiritual life and religion. Religion has been shown to be a powerful force for good in the lives of many people when the religion is inclusive, tolerant of other paths and emphasizes kindness, love, gratitude and forgiveness, as opposed to fear and judgment. Religions tend to have a particular set of ethics, customs, beliefs and ceremonies. All of this can be a wonderful means of sharing in a community of common faith. Have you been raised in a particular religion? If so, has it been meaningful to you? If it works for you, great. If not, you have the choice to keep seeking for a religious institution or a spiritual practice that is more comfortable for you, even if that means going your own way, separate from your family (which is hard, but doable). Visiting places of worship with friends or extended family members is a good way to broaden your spiritual horizons, and you just might find a spiritual home.

What places of worship/religions have you been exposed to or have you investigated?

_____

_____

_____

_____

_____

_____

Which of the above (if any) intrigued you or made you want to return?

_____

_____

_____

_____

_____

Religions typically provide a weekly spiritual practice of ceremony, prayer, inspirational messages, singing, etc. If it touches your heart, it is the easiest way to develop spiritual practice. If you decided to visit a religious service, write about what happened and how you felt about it.

_____

_____

_____

_____

Sadly, some people have been actively hurt by religion. If you experienced some form of abuse as a result of religion, please describe that here, as well as what sort of healing you have had from that experience.

_____

_____

_____

_____

If you experienced abuse as a result of religion and you have had no healing from that experience, what can you do now to heal that injury so that you can more easily explore this aspect of wellbeing?

_____

_____

_____

_____

_____

Spiritual practice set apart from a religion requires you to develop your own "church," with your own routine of meditation, prayer, ceremony or whatever you deem to be a regular part of your day/week. If this is your intention, please write your ideas about how you will develop a daily/weekly spiritual practice to develop your inner life.

_____

_____

_____

_____

_____

_____

_____

Religions and spiritual practices are culturally and developmentally diverse in faith, morality, values, ego, worldview, institutions and more, with far-reaching implications on values, behaviors and relationships. For many, spirituality takes the form of religious observance, prayer, meditation or a belief in a higher power. For others, it can be found in nature, music, art or a secular community. Spirituality is different for everyone. Watch out, though: When guilt, sin, shame and punishment are core themes, the health benefits are not realized. Positive thoughts bring positive practices, which bring positive habits.

Your deeply held beliefs strongly influence your health. So, take some time now to write about your religious or spiritual beliefs. Touch on what is most meaningful to you in this regard.

_____

_____

_____

_____

_____

_____

_____

_____

_____

_____

_____

_____

In the space below, use colored pencils or crayons to draw a picture of your concept of a Higher Power. Or, cut out pictures or words from magazines to place here to illustrate your Higher Power.

Possible Actions for Implementation

To foster spirituality in your lifestyle, examine your own values. Ask yourself:

1. What defines me as a person?

2. What role has religion or spirituality played in my life?

3. What is important to me?

4. How well do my daily activities reflect my values?

5. Do I neglect issues that matter to me because I'm busy spending time on things that matter less?

6. What are my important relationships?

7. What people give me a sense of community?

8. What/who inspires me and gives me hope?

9. What brings me joy?

10. What are my proudest achievements?

In the pages that follow, write about your answers to these questions. Take your time, as this is important.

_____

_____

_____

_____

_____

_____

_____

_____

_____

_____

_____

_____

_____

_____

_____

_____

Every one of the other seven Therapeutic Lifestyle Changes has an aspect of spiritual practice in it. Establishing healthy, loving relationships; spending time in and preserving the beauty of nature; conscious, sustainable eating; caring for the body through exercise and relaxation; enjoying laughter and fun; and doing for others all have spiritual components. Remembering the hopes and dreams you had before mental health challenges sidetracked you from your true self is part of your journey.

Forgiveness—including the willingness to forgive oneself and others—will make you less angry, more hopeful and better able to deal with emotions. Forgiveness reduces the build-up of stress hormones that accompany negative emotions like anger and resentment, and helps you maintain homeostasis. Who are the people in your life that you need to forgive? (Please don't confuse forgiveness with having to let destructive people back into your life. It simply means that you have let go of thoughts of resentment and revenge.)

_____

_____

_____

_____

_____

_____

_____

The power of prayer is widely practiced across all cultures. The act of putting oneself in the presence of your Higher Power is an important part of daily life. Prayer and meditation are particularly helpful tools for recovery and abstinence from addictive behaviors. When praying for yourself or others, an easy prayer goes like this:

May I be happy. May I be free from pain. May I be free. May I have all that I need to live my highest and best life.

To offer this prayer to others, insert their name(s) in the blank: *May _____ be happy. May _____ be free from pain. May _____ be free. May _____ have all that they need to live their highest and best life.*

You can, of course, pray the prayers of your religious faith, and you can make up your own. Use this space to write your own prayer.

_____

_____

_____

_____

_____

This search for meaning can be conducted on your own, as well as within a larger religious community, with friends, in therapy or with your family.

What would you like to say about your current understanding of your life's purpose—the reason you came here to planet Earth, and what you are meant to do with your life?

_____

_____

_____

_____

_____

Do you have spiritual beliefs, worries or concerns that are causing you stress? If so, please write about them here. These should be discussed with your group leader, your therapist or a spiritual adviser.

_____

_____

_____

_____

_____

Affirmations are a wonderful way to enhance your spiritual life. An affirmation is a positive statement made to draw positive energy into your thoughts and beliefs about yourself and your place in the world. When you have intention, fueled by affirmations and a plan of action, you are creating a directional compass. Here are a few affirmations you can use if you like them, and it's also good to create your own.

I am healthy in every possible way. I am physically healthy. I am mentally healthy. I am emotionally healthy. I am spiritually healthy. I am healthy in every possible way.

I am living my best life; striving for the highest and best use of my gifts and talents.

My relationships are loving and filled with kindness and respect.

I am grateful every day for me life.

Now that we've given you some examples, please write several of your own affirmations to be said daily.

_____

_____

_____

_____

_____

_____

Remember that the sweet territory of silent meditation is a wonderful addition to anyone's spiritual practice. When Mother Teresa was asked, "When you pray, what do you say to God?," she replied, "I don't talk. I simply listen." The interviewer then asked, "Ah, then, what is it that God says to you when you pray?" She replied, "He also doesn't talk. He also listens."

Sitting silently for 5–15 minutes each day and simply basking in the silence can be quite refreshing. It can also be very hard for a beginner. But, please try it. And, stay with it, even though it can be challenging. You'll get better at it and will come to enjoy the peace that comes as a result.

Try sitting in silence for 10 minutes and write about your experience.

_____

_____

_____

_____

_____

This chapter on spirituality would not be complete without the suggestion of a Gratitude Journal. Gratitude is a spiritual principle. Gratitude opens the heart and shifts the energy of challenging situations. You can write in your Gratitude Journal during your devotional time every day. Take pleasure in small things, like birds singing, as well as the larger WOW things in life. Make a note here about creating a Gratitude Journal if you don't already have one.

_____

_____

_____

_____

_____

Use this space to make a preliminary plan to make a religious or spiritual practice part of your everyday life. Comment on the time of day, what you will do, what supplies you might need, if others will be present or not and how long you will spend. Note which of the following possibilities you will include. Remember, this is a beginning plan, so make it doable for now and adjust it as time goes on.

- Attend faith-based service
- Meditate daily

- Practice yoga
- Join a choir
- Keep a Gratitude Journal
- Read a daily devotional
- Read scripture daily

Your Ideas

_____

_____

_____

_____

_____

_____

_____

_____

Benefits of Spirituality

- Gratitude
- Positivity and optimism
- Development of compassion
- Positive relationships
- A sense of purpose and meaning
- Character development
- A moral code
- Comfort in times of trouble

Final Words

"Health is a state of complete physical, mental and social wellbeing, and not merely the absence of disease or infirmity."
—World Health Organization

As with so many things in life, including recovery from mental health issues and addiction, the solutions are simple, but not necessarily easy. If you are reading these words, you have an understanding of what it means to apply Therapeutic Lifestyle Changes, as they have been presented here, to your program of recovery to optimize your mental health.

If you are recovering from substance abuse, obviously the first step was to become substance free. But that is just the beginning. If these other means of recovery, as outlined in this workbook, are neglected, a higher rate of relapse can be expected. Or, you might be substance free, but just not very happy and not operating optimally because your mental health has not been fully restored. The *8 Ways to Sustainable Wellbeing: For Teens and Their Families*, as outlined in this workbook, is the roadmap to optimize your mental health.

"Rome was not built in a day," as they say, and you are not likely to master all of these *8 Ways* in a short period of time. But, if you will continue to use this workbook, taking inventory of your progress from time to time, as you live your life in recovery, your mental health will definitely improve and your ability to stay disciplined about taking care of yourself will gradually get more efficient. It is truly the work of a lifetime.

One college student who came to Newport Academy for treatment was battling suicidal thoughts, depression, and anxiety. She felt lost, the simplest tasks seemed impossible and she even started pulling out her own hair, a condition known as trichotillomania.

Seeking treatment wasn't easy, but she says it saved her life, and she's stronger because of her struggles. Today, she's very involved in school and passionate about social justice and activism, and although she doesn't know exactly what her future holds, she knows that it will work out, because she is committed to her own wellbeing.

Like locusts, mental health challenges, including co-occurring issues such as substance abuse, can eat a wide swath through a teen's life, leaving ruins. There is a promise of restoration if you can just start on the path that has been laid out here.

Our wish for teens reading this book is that you take the time to heal and progress in all of these eight aspects of optimizing mental health, and that you are restored and continue restoring, so that you can enjoy your life to the fullest and be a blessing in the lives of others in your family and community, delivering your gifts and talents generously in the ways that only YOU can.

Good luck!

References

Alexander, C. & Langer, E. (1990). *Higher stages of human development*. New York: Oxford University Press.

Alexander, C. N., Rainforth, M. V., & Gelderloos, P. (1991). Transcendental meditation, self-actualization, and psychological health: A conceptual overview and statistical meta-analysis. *Journal of Social Behavior and Personality, 6*, 189-247.

Amminger, G.P., Schäfer, M.R., Papageorgiou, K., Klier, C.M., Cotton, S., Harrigan, S.M., ... Berger, G.E. (2010). Long-chain ω-3 fatty acids for indicated prevention of psychotic disorders: A randomized, placebo-controlled trial. *Archives of General Psychiatry, 67(2)*, 146-154.

Anderson, J., Liu, C. & Kryscio, R. (2008). Blood pressure response to transcendental meditation: A meta-analysis. *American Journal of Hypertension, 21*, 310-316.

Angell, M. (2009). Drug companies and doctors: A story of corruption. *The New York Review of Books, LVI (1)*, 8, 10, 12.

Anthes, E. (2009). Building around the mind. *Scientific American Mind, 20*, 52-59.

Appleton, K., Rogers, P. & Ness, A. (2010). Updated systematic review and meta-analysis of the effects of n-3 long-chain polyunsaturated fatty acids on depressed mood. *American Journal of Clinical Nutrition, 91(3)*, 757-770.

Arias, A. J., Steinberg, K., Banga, A., & Trestman, R. L. (2006). Systematic review of the efficacy of meditation techniques as treatments for medical illness. *The Journal of Alternative and Complementary Medicine, 12*, 817-832.

Barrett, W. (1962). *Irrational man: A study in existential philosophy*. New York, NY: Doubleday.

Berman, M., Jonides, J., & Kaplan, S. (2008). The cognitive benefits of interacting with nature. *Psychological Science, 19*, 1207-1212.

Bhandari, H. & Yasunobu, K. (2009). What is social capital? A comprehensive review of the concept. *Asian Journal of Social Science 37(3)*, 480-510.

Bjorklund, D. F. & Pellegrini, A. D. (2002). *The origins of human nature.* Washington DC: American Psychological Association.

Black, D. S., Milam, J., & Sussman, S. (2009). Sitting-meditation interventions among youth: A review of treatment efficacy. *Pediatrics, 124,* e532-e541.

Borgonovi, F. (2009). Doing well by doing good: The relationship between formal volunteering and self-reported happiness. *Social Science and Medicine, 66,* 2312-2334.

Brown, S., Nesse, R., Vinokur, A., & Smith, D. (2003). Providing social support may be more beneficial than receiving it. *Psychological Science, 14:* 320-327

Bracken, C., Skalski, P. (2010). Immersed in media: Telepresence in everyday life. New York: Routledge.

Buss, D. (2000). The evolution of happiness. *American psychologist, 55(1),* 15-23.

Cattaneo, L. & Rizzolatti, G. (2009). The mirror neuron system. *Archives of Neurology, 66(5),* 557-560.

Cherniak, E.P., Troen, B.R., Florez, H.J., Roos, B.A. & Levis, S. (2009). Some new food for thought: The role of vitamin D in the mental health of older adults. *Current Psychiatry Reports, 11(1),* 12-19. doi: 10.1007/s11920-009-0003-3

Chiesa, A. (2009). Zen meditation: An integration of current evidence. *Journal of Alternative and Complementary Medication, 15,* 585-592.

Chiesa, A. & Serretti, A. (2009) Mindfulness-based stress reduction for stress management in healthy people: A review and meta-analysis. *The Journal of Alternative and Complementary Medicine. 15(5),* 593-600. doi:10.1089/acm.2008.0495

Christakis, N.A. (2009). "You make me sick!" doi: 10.1136/bmj.b2739

Christofoletti, G., Oliani, M., Gobbi, S, & Stella, F. (2007). Effects of motor intervention in elderly patients with dementia: An analysis of randomized controlled trials. *Topics in Geriatric Rehabilitation, 23 (2),* 149- 154. doi: 10.1097/01.TGR.0000270183.90778.8e

Clark, C. & Stansfeld, S. (2007). The effect of transportation noise on health and cognitive development: A review of recent evidence. *International Journal of Comparative Psychology, (20),* 145-158.

Colcombe, S. & Kramer, A. F. (2003). Fitness effects on the cognitive function of older adults: A meta-analytic study. *Psychological Science, 14,* 125-130.

Cotman, C. & Berchtold, N. (2002). Exercise: A behavioral intervention to enhance brain health and plasticity. *Neuroscience, 25:* 295-301.

Cummins, R.A. (2005). The domains of life satisfaction: An attempt to order chaos. In A.C. Michalos (Ed.) *Citation Classics from Social Indicators Research*. (pp 559-584). Netherlands: Springer.

da Silva, T., Ravindran, L., & Ravindran, A. (2009). Yoga in the treatment of mood and anxiety disorders: A review. *Asian Journal of Psychiatry, 2,* 6-16.

Daley, A. J. (2002). Exercise therapy and mental health in clinical populations: Is exercise therapy a worthwhile intervention? *Advances in Psychiatric Treatment, 8:* 262-270.

Dawkins, R. (2006). *The God delusion.* Boston, MA: Houghton Mifflin.

Delpeuch, F., Marie, B., Monnnier, E., & Holdsworth, M. (2009). *Globesity: A planet out of control.* London: Earthscan Publications.

Deslandes, A., Moraes, H., Ferreira, C., Veiga, H., Silveria, H., Mouta, R., ...Laks, J. (2009). Exercise and mental health: Many reasons to move. *Neuropsychobiology, 59,* 191-198.

Devlin, A. & Arneill, A. (2003). Health care environments and patient outcomes: A review of the literature. *Environment and Behavior, 35,* 665.

Didonna, F. (Ed.). (2009). *Clinical handbook of mindfulness.* New York: Springer.

Dowd, S., Vickers, K., & Krahn, D. (2004). Exercise for depression. *Journal of Current Psychiatry, 3,* 10-20.

Duncan, B.L., Miller, S.O., Wampold, B.E. & Hubble, M.A. (Eds.). (2010). *The heart and soul of change: Delivering what works in therapy, 2*nd ed. Washington DC.: American Psychological Association.

Dunn, D., Aknin, L., & Norton, M. (2009). Spending money on others promotes happiness. *Science, 319,* 1687-1688.

Dusek, J., Otu, H., Wohlhueter, A., Zerbini, L., Joseph, M., Benson, H., ...Hasin, M. (2008). Genomic counter-stress changes induced by the relaxation response. *PLOS One, 3,* e2576.

Erikson, E. (1959). *Identity and the life cycle.* New York, NY: International University press.

Erikson, K. & Kramer, A. (2009). Aerobic exercise effects on cognitive and neural plasticity in older adults. *British Journal of Sports Medicine, 43,* 22-24.

Esbjorn-Hargens, S. & Zimmerman, M. (2009). *Integral ecology.* Boston: Integral Books.

Fischer, C. (2004). The 2004 GSS Finding of Shrunken Social Networks: An artifact? Published online by *American Sociological Review,* 74(4), 657-669. doi: 10.1177/000312240907400408

Fotuhi, M., Mohassel, P., & Yaffe, K. (2009). Fish consumption, long-chain omega-3 fatty acids and risk of cognitive decline or Alzheimer disease: A complex association. *Nature clinical practice.Neurology, 5,* 140-152.

Fowler, J. & Christakis, N. (2008). Dynamic spread of happiness in a large social network. *BMJ, 337:* a2338.

Fowler, J. & Christakis, N. (2010). Cooperative behavior cascades in human social networks. *Proceedings of the National Academy of Sciences, 107(12),* 5334-5338.

Fowler, J.W. (1995). *Stages of faith: The psychology of human development.* New York: HarperOne

Frattaroli, J., Weidner, G., Dnistrian, A., Kemp, C., Daubenmier, J., & Marlin, R. (2009). Clinical events in prostate cancer lifestyle trial: Results from two years of follow-up. *Urology, 72,* 1319-1323.

Fredrickson, B. (2002). Positive emotions. In C.Snyder & S. Lopez (Eds.), *Handbook of positive psychology* (pp. 120-134). New York, NY: Oxford University Press.

Freeman, M., Hibbeln, J., Wisner, K., Davis, J., Mischoulon, D., Peet, M., ...Stoll, A. (2006). Omega-3 fatty acids: Evidence basis for treatment and future research in psychiatry. *Journal of Clinical Psychiatry, 67,* 1954-1967.

Gebauer, J., Riketta, M., Broemer, P., & Mai, G. (2008). Pleasure and pressure based prosocial motivation: Divergent relations to subjective well-being. *Journal of Research in Personality, 42,* 399-420.

Gillies, P. (2007). Preemptive nutrition of pro-inflammatory states: A nutrigenomic model. *Nutritional Reviews, 65,* S217-S220.

Gomez-Pinilla, J. (2008). Brainfoods: The effect of nutrients on brain function. *Nature Reviews Neuroscience, 9,* 568-578.

Gopnik, A. (2008). Right again: The passions of John Stuart Mill. *The New Yorker,* October, 6, 85-91.

Gordon, D. (1999). The Epicurean option. *Philosophy Now, 24,* 33-35.

Gordon, G. & Esbjorn-Hargens, S. (2007). Integral play. *Journal of Integral Theory and Practice, 2,* 62-104.

Grimm, R., Spring, K., & Dietz, N. (2007). *The health benefits of volunteering: A review of recent research.* Washington, D.C.: Corporation for National and Community Service.

Gu, Y., Nieves, J.W., Stern, Y., Luchsinger, J.A. & Scarmeas, N. (2010). *Archives of Neurology, 67(6).* doi: 10.1001/archneurol.2010.84

Hamer, M. & Chida, Y. (2009). Physical activity and risk of neurodegenerative disease: a systematic review of prospective evidence. *Psychological Medicine, 39,* 3-11.

Hamer, M. & Chida, Y. (2008). Exercise and depression: A meta-analysis and critical review. In W.Hansson & E. Olsson (Eds.). *New perspectives on women and depression* (pp. 255-266). New York: Nova Science Publishers Inc.

Harris, S. (2005). *The End of Faith*. New York, NY: W.W. Norton.

Hertzog, C., Kramer, A., Wilson, R., & Lindenberger, U. (2009). Fit body, fit mind? *Scientific American Mind, 20,* 24-31.

Higgins, S., Hall, E., Wall, K., Woolner, P., & McCaughey, C. (2005). The impact of school environments: A literature review. http://www.cfbt.com/PDF/91085.pdf

Hitchens, C. (2007). *God is not great.* New York, NY: Twelve Books.

Ho, C., Payne, L., Orsega-Smith, E., & Godby, G. (2003). Parks, recreation, and public health. *Parks & Recreation, 38,* 18, 20-27.

Hoffman, S.G., Sawyer, A.T., Witt, A.A. & Oh, D. (2010). The effect of mindfulness-based therapy on anxiety and depression: A meta-analytic review. *Journal of Consulting Clinical Psychology, 78(2),* 169-183. doi: 10.1037/a0018555

Hopkins, J. (2001). *Cultivating compassion.* New York, NY: Broadway Books.

Innis, S. M. (2009). Omega-3 fatty acids and neural development to two years of age. *Journal of Pediatric Gastroenterology and Nutrition, 48,* S16-S24.

Ito, M., Horst, H., Brittani, M., Boyd, D., Herr-Stephenson, B., Lang, P., ...Robinson, L. (2008). *Living and learning with new media: Summary of findings from the digital youth project.* Cambridge: The MIT Press.

Jetten, J., Haslam, C., Haslam, S., & Branscombe, N. (2009). The social cure. *Scientific American Mind, 20,* 26-33.

Kang, J. H., Ascherio, A., & Groodstein, F. (2005). Fruit and vegetable consumption and cognitive decline in aging women. *Annals of Neurology, 57,* 713-720.

Kessler, D. (2009). *The end of overeating.* New York, NY: Rodale Press.

Khaw, K. T., Wareham, N., Bingham, S., Welch, A., & Luben, R. (2008). Combined impact of health behaviors and mortality in men and women. *Obstetrical & Gynecological Survey, 63,* 376-377.

Kirkwood, G., Rampes, H., Tuffrey, V., Richardson, J., & Pilkington, K. (2005). Yoga for anxiety: A systematic review of the research evidence. *British Journal of Sports Medicine, 39,* 884-891.

Koenig, H. (2002). *Spirtuality in patient care.* Philadelphia, PA: Templeton Foundation Press.

Koenig, H. G. (2009). Research on religion, spirituality, and mental health: A review. *Canadian Journal of Psychiatry, 54,* 283-291.

Koenig, H. G., McCullough, M. E., & Larson, D. B. (2001). *Handbook of religion and health.* Oxford University Press.

Kraguljac, N.V., Montori, V.M., Pavuluri, M., Chai, H.S., Wilson, B.S. & Unal, S.S. (2009). Efficacy of omega-3 fatty acids in mood disorders - a systematic review and metaanalysis. *Psychopharmaology Bulletin, 42(3),* 39-54.

Kuller, R., Ballal, S., Laike, T., Mikellides, B., & Tonello, G. (2006). The impact of light and colour on psychological mood: A cross-cultural study of indoor work environments. *Ergonomics, 49*, 1496-1507.

Kuramoto, A. (2006). Therapeutic benefits of Tai Chi exercise: Research review. *Wisconsin Medical Journal, 105*, 42-46.

Langerok, H. (1915). A study of professional deformation. *The American Journal of Sociology, 21*, 30-34.

Larun, L., Nordeim, L., Ekeland, E., Hagen, K., & Heian, F. (2006). Exercise in prevention and treatment of anxiety and depression among children and young people. *Cochrane Database of Systematic Reviews.* http://www2.cochrane.org/reviews/en/ab004691.html

Lester, S. & Russell, W. (2008). *Play for a change - play, policy and practice: A review of contemporary perspectives.* London: National Children's Bureau.

Lefcourt, H. (2002). Humor. In C.Snyder & S. Lopez (Eds.), *Handbook of positive psychology* (pp. 619-631). New York, NY: Oxford University Press.

Lin, P. & Su, K. (2007). A meta-analytic review of double-blind, placebo-controlled trials of antidepressant efficacy of omega-3 fatty acids. *Journal of Clinical Psychiatry, 68*, 1056-1061.

Lipton, L. (2008). Using yoga to treat disease: An evidence based review. *Journal of the American Academy of Physician Assistants, 21*, 34, 36, 38, 41.

Long, B. J., Calfas, K. J., Wooten, W., Sallis, J. F., Patrick, K., Goldstein, M., ...Heath, G.. (1996). A multisite field test of the acceptability of physical activity counseling in primary care: Project PACE. *American Journal of Preventative Medicine, 12*, 73-81.

Louve, R. (2005). *Last child in the woods: Saving our children from nature-deficit disorder.* Chapel Hill, NC: Algonquin Books of Chapel Hill.

Luhrmann, T. M. (2001). *Of two minds: An anthropologist looks at American psychiatry.* New York, NY: Vintage.

Maller, C., Townsend, M., Pryor, A., Brown, P., & Sleger, L. (2006). Healthy nature, healthy people: 'Contact with nature' as an upstream health promotion intervention for populations. *Health Promotion International, 21*, 45-54.

Manzoni, G. M., Pagnini, F., Castelnuovo, G., & Molinari, E. (2008). Relaxation training for anxiety: a ten-year sytematic review with meta-analysis. *BMC Psychiatry, 8*, 1-12.

Mares, M.L. & Woodard, E. (2005). Positive effects of television on children's social interactions: A meta-analysis. *MediaPsychology, 7(3)*, 301-322.

McEntee, D. & Halgin, R. (1996). Therapists' attitudes about addressing the role of exercise in psychotherapy. *Journal of Clinical Psychology, 52*, 48-60.

McMorris, T., Tomporowski, P. & Audiffren, M. (2009). *Exercise and cognitive function.* Chichester, England: Wiley-Blackwell

McPherson, M., Smith-Lovin, L. & Brashears, M.E. (2006). Social isolation in America: Changes in core discussion networks over two decades. *American Sociological Review, 71(3),* 353-375. doi: 10.1177/000312240607100301

Mojtabai, R. & Olfson, M. (2008). National trends in psychotherapy by office-based psychiatrists. *Archives of General Psychiatry, 65,* 962-970.

Montanye, J. A. (2001). Bowling alone: The collapse and revival of an American community. *The Independent Review, 5(3).* http://www.independent.org/publications/tir/article.asp?a=205

Morris, M., Evans, D., Tangney, C., Bienias, J., & Wilson, R. (2006). Associations of vegetable and fruit consumption with age-related cognitive change. *Neurology, 67:* 1370-1376.

Noaghuil, S. & Hibbeln, J. (2003). Cross-national comparisons of seafood consumption and rates of bipolar disorder. *American Journal of Psychiatry, 160,* 2222-2227.

Norcross, J. (2010). The therapeutic relationship. In B. Duncan, S. Miller, B. Wampold, M. Hubble, M. (Eds.). *The heart and soul of change: Delivering what works in therapy, 2nd ed.* (pp. 113-142).Washington, DC: American Psychological Association.

Oken, E., Radesky, J. S., Wright, R. O., Bellinger, D. C. & Chitra, J., Amarasiriwardena, ... Gillman, M.W. (2008). Maternal fish intake during pregnancy, blood mercury levels, and child cognition at age 3 years in a U.S. cohort. *American Journal of Epidemiology, 167,* 1171-1181.

Ornish, D., Lin, J., Daubenmier, J., Weidner, G., Epel, E., Kemp, C., ...Carroll, P. (2008). Increased telomerase activity and comprehensive lifestyle changes: A pilot study. *The Lancet Oncology, 9,* 1048-1057.

Ospina, M. B., Bond, T. K., Karkhaneh, M., Tjosvold, L., Vandermeer, B. & Liang, Y....Klassen, T.P. (2007). *Meditation practices for health: State of the research.* AHRQ Publication No.07-E010. http://www.ahrq.gov/downloads/pub/evidence/pdf/meditation/medit.pdf

Pagnoni, G. & Cekic, M. (2007). Age effects on gray matter volume and attentional performance in Zen meditation. *Neurobiological Aging, 28,* 1623-627.

Pilgrim, D., Rogers, A., & Bentall, R. (2009). The centrality of personal relationships in the creation and amelioration of mental health problems: The current interdisciplinary case. *Health: An interdisciplinary Journal for the Social Study of Health, Illness & Medicine, 13,* 235.

Pilkington, K., Kirkwood, G., Rampes, H., & Richardson, J. (2005). Yoga for depression: The research evidence. *Journal of Affective Disorders, 89,* 13-24.

Pischke, C.R., Scherwitz, L.,Weidner, G. & Ornish, D. (2008). Long-term effects of lifestyle changes on well-being and cardiac variables among coronary heart disease patients. *Health psychology, 27(5)*, 584-592. doi: 10.1037/0278-6133.27.5.584

Post, S. (2007). *The science of altruism and health.* New York: Oxford Press.

Post, S. & Niemark, J. (2007). *Why good things happen to good people.* New York: Broadway Books.

Post, S., Underwood, L., Schloss, J., & Hulbert, W. (2002). *Altruism and altruistic love: Science, philosophy and religion in dialogue.* Oxford: Oxford University Press.

Preiss, R.W., Gayle, B.M., Burrell, N., Allen, M. & Bryant, J. (2006). *Mass media effects research: Advances through meta-analysis.* New York: Routledge Press.

Prolla, T. A. & Mattson, M. P. (2001). Molecular mechanisms of brain aging and neurodegenerative disorders: Lessons from dietary restriction. *Trends in Neurosciences, 24*, s21-s31.

Pryor, A., Townsend, M., Maller, C., & Field, K. (2006). Health and well-being naturally: 'Contact with nature' in health promotion for targeted individuals, communities and populations. *Health Promotion Journal of Australia, 17*, 114-223.

Putnam, R. D. (1995). Bowling alone: America's declining social capital. *Journal of Democracy, 6*, 65-78.

Putnam, R. D. (2000). *Bowling alone: The collapse and revival of American community.* New York: Simon Schuster.

Quaney, B.M., Boyd, L.A., McDown, J.M., Zahner, L.H., Jianghua, He, Mayo, M.S. & Macko, R.F. (2009). Aerobic exercise improves cognition and motor function poststroke. Neurorehabilitation and Neural Repair, 23(9), 879-885. doi: 10.1177/1545968309338193

Raji, C., Ho, A., Neelroop, P., Becker, J., Lopez, O., & Kuller, L. (2009). Brain structure and obesity. *Neuroimage, 47, (Supplement 1)*, S39-S41.

Rusbult, C, Finkel, E. & Kumashiro, M. The Michelangelo phenomenon. *Current Directions in Psychological Science, 18(6)*, 305-309.

Sarris, J., Schoendorfer, N., & Kavanagh, D. J. (2009). Major depressive disorder and nutritional medicine. *Nutrition Reviews, 67*, 125-131.

Shapiro, S. & Carlson, L. (2009). *The art and science of mindfulness.* Washington D.C.: American Psychological Association Press.

Shedler, J.K. (2010). "The efficacy of psychodynamic psychotherapy." *American Psychologist, 65(2)*, 98-109.

Sidhu, K., Vandana, P., & Balon, R. (2009). Exercise prescription: A practical effective therapy for depression. *Current Psychiatry, 8*, 39-51.

Small, G. & Vorgan, G. (2008). Meet your ibrain. *Scientific American Mind, 19,* 42-49.

Smith, E. (2000). *The body in psychotherapy.* Jefferson, N.C.: McFarland & Company.

Sofi, F., Cesari, F., Abbate, R., Gensini, G.F. & Casini, A. (2008). Adherence to Mediterranean diet and health status: meta-analysis. doi: 10.1136/bmj.a1344

Song, C. & Zhao, S. (2008). Omega-3 fatty acid eicosapentaenoic acid: A new treatment for psychiatric and neurodegenerative diseases. *Expert Opinion on Investigational Drugs, 16,* 1627-1638.

Stahl, L., Begg, D., Weisinger, R., & Sinclair, A. (2008). The role of omega-3 fatty acids in mood disorders. *Current Opinion in Investigational Drugs, 9,* 57-64.

Stathopoulou, G., Powers, M., Berry, A., Smits, J., & Otto, M. (2006). Exercise interventions for mental health: A quantitative and qualitative review. *Clinical Psychology: Science and Practice, 13,* 179-193.

Stranahan, A.M., Khalil, D. & Gould, E. (2006). Social isolation delays the positive effects of running on adult neurogenesis. *Nature Neuroscience, 9,* 526-533. doi: 10.1038/nn1668

Sui, X., Laditka, J., Church, T., Hardin, J., Chase, N., Davis, K. & Blair, S. (2009). Prospective study of cardiorespiratory fitness and depressive symptoms in women and men. *Journal of Psychiatric Research, 43,* 546-552.

Taylor, A. F. & Kuo, F. E. (2009). Children with attention deficits concentrate better after walk in the park. *Journal of Attention Disorders, 12,* 402-409.

Taylor, A. F., Kuo, F. E., & Sullivan, W. C. (2001). Coping with ADD: The surprising connection to green play settings. *Environment and Behavior, 33,* 54-77.

Thoreau, H. (1854). *Walden; or life in the woods.* Boston, MA: Ticknor & Fields.

Thoreau, H. (1921). *A week on the Concord and Merimack Rivers.* New York: Charles Scribner & Sons.

Tiffin, J. & Terashima, N. (2001). *HyperReality: Paradigm for the third millennium.* New York, NY: Routledge.

Trakhtenberg, E. (2008). The effects of guided imagery on the immune system: A critical review. *International Journal of Neuroscience, 118,* 839-855.

Ulrich, R. (2006). Evidence-based health care architecture. *The Lancet, 368:* 538-539.

Voren, R. V. (2002). Comparing Soviet and Chinese political psychiatry. *Journal of the American Academy of Psychiatry and the Law, 30,* 131-135.

Walsh, R. (1999). *Essential spirituality: The seven central practices.* New York: Wiley & Sons.

Walsh, R. The state of the integral enterprise, Part I: Current status, possible applications, and potential traps. *Journal of Integral Theory and Practice,* 4(3), 1-12, 2009.

Walsh, R. Contemplative psychotherapies. In R. Corsini & Wedding (Eds.) *Current psychotherapies (9th ed.)*. Belmont, CA: Thomson, in press.

Walsh, R. & Shapiro, S. (2006). The meeting of meditative disciplines and Western psychology: A mutually enriching dialogue. *American Psychologist, 61*, 227-239.

Wang, W., Zhang, A., Rasmussen, B., Lin, L., Dunning, T., Kang, S., ...Lo, S.K. (2009). The effect of Tai chi on psychosocial well-being: A systematic review of randomized controlled trials. *Journal of Acupuncture and Meridian Studies, 2*, 171-181.

Wehrenberg, M. & Coppersmith, L. (2008). Technotrap: When work becomes your second home. *Psychotherapy Networker, 32(2)*, 40-45,64.

WHO (2008). Controlling the global obesity epidemic. http://www.who.int/nutrition/topics/obesity/en/index.html

Wilber, K. (2000). *Integral psychology*. Boston: Shambhala.

Wilber, K. (2005). *A sociable God*. Boston: Shambhala.

Wilber, K. (2006). *Integral spirituality*. Boston: Shambhala.

Willis, L. M., Shukitt-Hale, B., & Joseph, J. A. (2009). Recent advances in berry supplementation and age related cognitive decline. *Current Opinion in Clinical Nutrition & Metabolic Care, 12*, 91-94.

Wolf, P., Beiser, A., Elias, M., Au, R., Vasan, R., & Seshradi, S. (2007). Relations to obesity in cognitive function: The Framingham heart study. *Current Alzheimer Research, 4*, 111-116.

Wordsworth.W. (1998). *The collected poems of William Wordsworth*. Hertfordshire, Great Britain: Wordsworth Editions Ltd.

Xiong, G. L. & Doraiswamy, P. M. (2009). Does meditation enhance cognition and brain plasticity? *Annals of the New York Academy of Sciences, 1172*, 63-69.

Yalom, I. (2002). *The gift of therapy*. New York: Harper Collins.

About the Authors

Dr. Sonnee Weedn is a clinical and forensic psychologist, an APA-certified specialist in the treatment of alcoholism and other chemical dependencies, and an Advanced EM.D.R practitioner. She began her practice in 1980 when Vietnam veterans were beginning to manifest symptoms of trauma and substance abuse. It was with them that she learned to treat the dual diagnosis of PTSD and chemical dependency. She treats individuals, couples and families; maintains long-term therapy groups; and coaches executives and athletes. She has conducted trainings in group psychotherapy, spirituality for recovering people, treatment for psychological trauma and other topics at conferences and events around the world.

As the founder of the Sonnee Weedn Institute for Integrative Therapies, she has received funding for various educational enterprises, particularly those that emphasize cross- cultural bridgework, including collaborations with Dr. Ysaye Barnwell, founding member of the a capella group Sweet Honey in the Rock; Native Americans Albert Sombrero and Lorenzo Archuleta; Tibetan Buddhist monk Lama Tenzin Choegyal; and the Medium of the State Oracle of Tibet, Ven. Thupten Ngodup. In 2015 and 2016, she was an invited speaker for His Holiness, the Dalai Lama's *Mind, Body, Life Conference* in Dharmsala, India. It was for these presentations that she became familiar with the research of Roger Walsh, M.D., PhD, into Therapeutic Lifestyle Change for optimizing mental health.

Dr. Weedn won the Clark Vincent Award, given by the California Association of Marriage and Family Therapists, for her contributions to the textbook *Making Advances: A Comprehensive Treatment Guide for Female Sex and Love Addicts*. For her award-winning book, *Many Blessings: A Tapestry of Accomplished African American Women*, she interviewed and wrote the life stories of 30 resilient and resourceful contemporary African American women, including the former U.S. Surgeon General, Dr. Joycelyn Elders; actress Loretta Devine; Fulbright scholar Dr. Valata Jenkins-Monroe; and NASA astronaut Col. (ret.) Yvonne Cagle, M.D., who invited her to become a founding member and chairman of the Deep Space Research–2030 Consortium, researching behavioral health protocols for astronauts going to Mars in the future. Currently, she works with neuro-engineer Dr. Curtis Cripe, repairing the neurological/cognitive damage done by substance abuse or head trauma, and maintains privileges at Hoag Hospital Newport Beach in California.

Jamison Monroe is the Founder and Executive Chairman of Newport Healthcare, dedicated to bringing teens and young adults from self-destruction to self-esteem by treating the trauma and attachment wounds underlying mental health and co-occurring disorders. He brings years of both professional and personal recovery experience to his leadership. A prominent voice in the field of adolescent mental health, and an active participant in the movement to reduce the stigma around mental health and substance abuse challenges, Jamison testified before England's Parliament on the subject of teen prescription drug abuse and gave the keynote address at the United Kingdom and European Symposium on Addictive Disorders. He is the recipient of the Freedom Institute's 2014 Mona Mansell Award for his indelible impact on the recovery field and community.

Jamison founded Newport Academy in 2008 to treat clients ages 12–20 suffering from primary mental health issues. He then evolved his vision, translating the highly successful Newport Academy model into a program for 18- to 27-year-olds. Newport Institute takes into account the unique needs of young adults, while maintaining the core philosophies that underlie Newport's integrated treatment model—providing clinical excellence, a wide range of evidence-based therapeutic modalities, and the practical skills necessary to build a fulfilling life. Guided by rigorous third-party research tracking patient outcomes, Newport Academy and Newport Institute continue to achieve industry-leading rates of treatment success.

Prior to founding Newport, Jamison worked in multiple mental health and co-occurring disorder treatment facilities—starting his career as an overnight coordinator and working his way up to Executive Director. He is also the co-founder of Drugs over Dinner, advocating open conversation about drug use in families and communities. Jamison was a producer of the critically acclaimed documentary film *Behind the Orange Curtain*, about the prescription drug epidemic in the United States. He is also a writer, a frequent contributor to numerous media outlets, and a certified teacher of yoga and meditation.

Worksheets

Life Assessment

NAME_____ DATE_____

Healthy habits can give you the life you want. As you work on building a healthy future for yourself, periodically take a moment to assess what you like and dislike about all areas of your life. Rate each on a 1-5 scale, with 5 being most satisfied and 1 indicating a lot of improvement is needed. Begin making changes in the lowest scored areas and set goals and action plan to work on.

1. Health & Wellness   _____

2. Lifestyle & Fun   _____

3. School & Academics   _____

4. Family & Friends   _____

5. Dating & Relationships   _____

6. Money & Finances   _____

7. Career Planning   _____

8. Spirituality   _____

Support Group

NAME _____ DATE _____

Today	In The Future
PROFESSIONALS (therapist, psychiatrist, lawyer, physician, trainer, job counselor, spiritual advisor) 1. _____ 2. _____ 3. _____ 4. _____	PROFESSIONALS (job counselor, therapist, psychiatrist, lawyer, physician, trainer, spiritual advisor) 1. _____ 2. _____ 3. _____ 4. _____
FAMILY (parents, siblings, relatives) 1. _____ 2. _____ 3. _____ 4. _____	**FAMILY** (parents, siblings, relatives) 1. _____ 2. _____ 3. _____ 4. _____
FRIENDS 1. _____ 2. _____ 3. _____ 4. _____	**FRIENDS** 1. _____ 2. _____ 3. _____ 4. _____
OTHER SUPPORT (teacher, neighbor, 12-Step group, sponsor, religious leader, advisor) 1. _____ 2. _____ 3. _____ 4. _____	**OTHER SUPPORT** (teacher, neighbor, 12-Step group, sponsor, religious leader, advisor) 1. _____ 2. _____ 3. _____ 4. _____
PETS 1. _____ 2. _____ 3. _____ 4. _____	PETS 1. _____ 2. _____ 3. _____ 4. _____

Stressor Worksheet

NAME_____ DATE_____

- List the triggers that make you uncomfortable, reduce your functioning and/or cause you to be tempted to relapse or act out in some way that is destructive to you or others.

- Write down the people, situations, times, places and/or events that trigger unhealthy thoughts and behaviors.

- Then, write down how you plan to respond differently with healthy thinking and activities.

WHO	
WHAT	
WHERE	
WHEN	
WHY	
-HOW-	
WHO	
WHAT	
WHERE	
WHEN	
WHY	
-HOW-	
WHO	
WHAT	
WHERE	
WHEN	
WHY	
-HOW-	

Stressor Worksheet

NAME_____ DATE_____

- List the triggers that make you uncomfortable, reduce your functioning, and/or cause you to be tempted to relapse or behave in ways you regret.

- Write down the people, situations, times, places and/or events that trigger unhealthy thoughts and behaviors.

- Then, write down how you plan to respond differently with healthy thinking and activities.

WHO	
WHAT	
WHERE	
WHEN	
WHY	
-HOW-	
WHO	
WHAT	
WHERE	
WHEN	
WHY	
-HOW-	
WHO	
WHAT	
WHERE	
WHEN	
WHY	
-HOW-	

Progress Charts & Journal

CALL TO ACTION

Today, I will _____

_____

_____

_____

_____

_____

This week, I will _____

_____

_____

_____

_____

_____

_____

This month, I will _____

_____

_____

_____

_____

_____

_____

Habit Change Worksheet

TRIGGER	ROUTINE ACTION	REWARD

TRIGGER Identification

Item	Day 1	Day 2	Day 3
Where are you?			
What time is it?			
What is your emotional state?			
Who else is around?			
What action preceded it?			

Weekly Action Plan

This week, I will take care of my body by: _____
_____
_____
_____

This week, I will take care of my mind by: _____
_____
_____
_____

This week, I will take care of my spirit by: _____
_____
_____
_____

This week, I will take care of my relationships by: _____
_____
_____
_____

This week, I will take care of my environment by: _____
_____
_____
_____

Nutrition Goal-Setting Worksheet

NAME_____ DATE_____

My Nutrition Goal is: _____

_____

_____

_____

Goal Completion Date: _____

I will know I have reached my goal because: _____

_____

_____

Three things that will help me reach my goal:

1 _____

2 _____

3 _____

Two people who can help me reach my goal:

1 _____

2 _____

Steps to reaching my goal: _____

_____

_____

_____

_____

_____

Food Journal

NAME_____ WEEK_____

MEAL/ SNACK	TIME	FOOD	BEVERAGE
Breakfast			
Morning Snack			
Lunch			
Afternoon Snack			
Dinner			
Evening Snack			

Nutrition Facts Label

What's On The Nutrition Facts Label

The Nutrition Facts Label found on packaged foods and beverages is your daily tool for making informed food choices that contribute to healthy lifelong eating habits. Explore it today and discover the wealth of information it contains!

Serving Size

Serving Size is based on the **amount of food that is customarily eaten** at one time. All of the nutrition information listed on the Nutrition Facts Label is based on **one serving** of the food.

The serving size is shown as a common household measure that is appropriate to the food (such as cup, tablespoon, piece, slice, or jar), followed by the metric amount in grams (g).

When comparing calories and nutrients in different foods, check the serving size in order to make an accurate comparison.

Servings Per Container

Servings Per Container shows the **total number of servings** in the entire food package or container. It is common for one package of food to contain more than one serving.

The information listed on the Nutrition Facts Label is based on **one serving**. So, if a package contains *two servings* and you eat the entire package, you have consumed *twice the amount of calories and nutrients* listed on the label.

Calories

Calories refers to the **total number of calories**, or "energy," supplied from all sources (fat, carbohydrate, protein, and alcohol) in one serving of the food.

To achieve or maintain a healthy body weight, balance the number of calories you eat and drink with the number of calories you burn during physical activity and through your body's metabolic processes.

As a general rule:
100 calories per serving is **moderate**
400 calories per serving is **high**

Nutrition Facts

Serving Size 1 package (272g)
Servings Per Container 1

Amount Per Serving

Calories 300   Calories from Fat 45

	% Daily Value*
Total Fat 5g	**8%**
Saturated Fat 1.5g	**8%**
Trans Fat 0g	
Cholesterol 30mg	**10%**
Sodium 430mg	**18%**
Total Carbohydrate 55g	**18%**
Dietary Fiber 6g	**24%**
Sugars 23g	
Protein 14g	
Vitamin A	80%
Vitamin C	35%
Calcium	6%
Iron	15%

* Percent Daily Values are based on a 2,000 calorie diet. Your Daily Values may be higher or lower depending on your calorie needs:

	Calories:	2,000	2,500
Total Fat	Less than	65g	80g
Saturated Fat	Less than	20g	25g
Cholesterol	Less than	300mg	300mg
Sodium	Less than	2,400mg	2,400mg
Total Carbohydrate		300g	375g
Dietary Fiber		25g	30g

Tip: "Fat-free" doesn't mean "calorie-free." Some lower fat food items may have as many calories as the full-fat version. Always check the Nutrition Facts Label and compare the calories and nutrients in the fat-free version to the regular version.

Calories from Fat

Calories from Fat are *not* additional calories, but are **fat's contribution to the total number of calories** in one serving of the food. The Nutrition Facts Label lists the calories from fat because fat has more than *twice* the number of calories per gram than carbohydrate or protein.

For example, if the Nutrition Facts Label says one serving of food contains 150 calories and 100 calories from fat, the remaining 50 calories comes from carbohydrate, protein, and/or alcohol.

 http://www.fda.gov/nutritioneducation   **What's On The Nutrition Facts Label 1**

Percent Daily Value (%DV)

Percent Daily Value (%DV) shows **how much of a nutrient is in one serving** of the food. The %DVs are based on the Daily Values for key nutrients, which are the amounts (in grams, milligrams, or micrograms) of nutrients recommended per day for Americans 4 years of age and older. The %DV column doesn't add up vertically to 100%. Instead, the %DV is the percentage of the Daily Value for each nutrient in one serving of the food.

For example, the Daily Value for saturated fat is 20 grams (g), which equals 100% DV. If the Nutrition Facts Label says one serving of a food contains 1.5 g of saturated fat, then the %DV for saturated fat for this specific food is 8%. That means the food contains 8% of the maximum amount of saturated fat that an average person should eat in an entire day.

Using the %DV

Compare Foods: Use the %DV to compare food products (remember to make sure the serving size is the same) and to choose products that are higher in nutrients you want to get more of and lower in nutrients you want to get less of.

As a general rule:
5% **DV** or less of a nutrient per serving is **low**
20% **DV** or more of a nutrient per serving is **high**

Understand Nutrient Content Claims: Use the %DV to help distinguish one claim from another, such as "light," "low," and "reduced." Simply compare the %DVs in each food product to see which one is higher or lower in a particular nutrient; there is no need to memorize definitions.

Manage "Dietary Trade-Offs": Use the %DV to make dietary trade-offs with other foods throughout the day. You don't have to give up a favorite food to eat a healthy diet. When a food you like is high in a nutrient you want to get less of – or low in a nutrient you want to get more of – balance it with foods that are low (or high) in that nutrient at other times of the day.

Nutrition Facts

Serving Size 1 package (272g)
Servings Per Container 1

Amount Per Serving

Calories 300 — Calories from Fat 45

	% Daily Value*
Total Fat 5g	**8%**
Saturated Fat 1.5g	**8%**
Trans Fat 0g	
Cholesterol 30mg	**10%**
Sodium 430mg	**18%**
Total Carbohydrate 55g	**18%**
Dietary Fiber 6g	**24%**
Sugars 23g	
Protein 14g	
Vitamin A	80%
Vitamin C	35%
Calcium	6%
Iron	15%

* Percent Daily Values are based on a 2,000 calorie diet. Your Daily Values may be higher or lower depending on your calorie needs:

	Calories:	2,000	2,500
Total Fat	Less than	65g	80g
Saturated Fat	Less than	20g	25g
Cholesterol	Less than	300mg	300mg
Sodium	Less than	2,400mg	2,400mg
Total Carbohydrate		300g	375g
Dietary Fiber		25g	30g

Footnote

The Asterisk

The asterisk (*) following the heading "% Daily Value" on the Nutrition Facts Label refers to the standard footnote at the bottom of all labels, which specifies that some of the %DVs are based on a **2,000 calorie daily diet**. A 2,000 calorie daily diet is often used as the basis for general nutrition advice; however, your Daily Values may be higher or lower depending on your calorie needs. Calorie needs vary according to age, gender, height, weight, and physical activity level. Check your calorie needs at http://www.choosemyplate.gov.

Daily Value Recommendations

If there is enough space available on the food package, the footnote on the Nutrition Facts Label will also list the **Daily Values** for some key nutrients. These are given for both a 2,000 and 2,500 calorie daily diet. This section also includes **goals** regarding how much or how little of a nutrient to aim for in your daily diet. The Daily Values for some nutrients are different for a 2,000 or 2,500 calorie diet, while others (cholesterol and sodium) remain the same for both calorie amounts.

What's On The Nutrition Facts Label 2

Nutrients

The Nutrition Facts Label can help you learn about the **nutrient content** of many foods in your diet. It also enables you to compare foods to make healthy choices.

The Nutrition Facts Label must list: total fat, saturated fat, *trans* fat, cholesterol, sodium, total carbohydrate, dietary fiber, sugars, protein, vitamin A, vitamin C, calcium, and iron.

The Nutrition Facts Label may also list: monounsaturated fat, polyunsaturated fat, soluble fiber, insoluble fiber, sugar alcohol, other carbohydrate, vitamins (such as biotin, folate, niacin, riboflavin, pantothenic acid, thiamin, vitamin B_6, vitamin B_{12}, vitamin D, vitamin E, and vitamin K) and minerals (such as chromium, copper, iodine, magnesium, manganese, molybdenum, phosphorus, potassium, selenium, and zinc).

Nutrients to get less of – get less than 100% DV of these each day: saturated fat, *trans* fat, cholesterol, and sodium. (Note: *trans* fat has no %DV, so use the amount of grams as a guide)

Nutrients to get more of – get 100% DV of these on most days: dietary fiber, vitamin A, vitamin C, calcium, and iron.

Nutrition Facts

Serving Size 1 package (272g)
Servings Per Container 1

Amount Per Serving

Calories 300 — Calories from Fat 45

	% Daily Value*
Total Fat 5g	8%
Saturated Fat 1.5g	8%
Trans Fat 0g	
Cholesterol 30mg	10%
Sodium 430mg	18%
Total Carbohydrate 55g	18%
Dietary Fiber 6g	24%
Sugars 23g	
Protein 14g	
Vitamin A	80%
Vitamin C	35%
Calcium	6%
Iron	15%

* Percent Daily Values are based on a 2,000 calorie diet. Your Daily Values may be higher or lower depending on your calorie needs:

		Calories:	2,000	2,500
Total Fat	Less than		65g	80g
Saturated Fat	Less than		20g	25g
Cholesterol	Less than		300mg	300mg
Sodium	Less than		2,400mg	2,400mg
Total Carbohydrate			300g	375g
Dietary Fiber			25g	30g

Ingredient List

The Ingredient List shows each ingredient in a food by its **common or usual name in descending order** by weight. So, the ingredient with the greatest contribution to the product weight is listed first, and the ingredient contributing the least by weight is listed last. The ingredient list is usually located near the name of the food's manufacturer and often below the Nutrition Facts Label.

Use this list to find out whether a food or beverage contains ingredients that are sources of nutrients you want to get less of, such as saturated fat (like shortening), *trans* fat (like partially hydrogenated oils), and added sugars (like syrups) – and sources of nutrients you want to get more of, such as whole grains (like whole oats).

INGREDIENTS: WHOLE WHEAT PASTA (WATER, WHOLE WHEAT FLOUR), COOKED WHITE MEAT CHICKEN (WHITE MEAT CHICKEN, WATER, MODIFIED TAPIOCA STARCH, CHICKEN FLAVOR [DRIED CHICKEN BROTH, CHICKEN POWDER, NATURAL FLAVOR], CARRAGEENAN, WHEY PROTEIN CONCENTRATE, SOYBEAN OIL, CORN SYRUPSOLIDS, SODIUM PHOSPHATE, SALT), WATER, CARROTS, GREEN BEANS, APPLE JUICE CONCENTRATE, DRIED CRANBERRIES (CRANBERRIES, SUGAR, SUNFLOWER OIL), APPLES (APPLES, CITRIC ACID, SALT, WATER), CONTAINS 2% OR LESS OF: BUTTER (CREAM, SALT), MODIFIED CORNSTARCH, CHICKEN BROTH, ORANGE JUICE CONCENTRATE, APPLE CIDER VINEGAR, SUGAR, SOYBEAN OIL, SEA SALT, GINGER PUREE (GINGER, WATER, CITRIC ACID), YEAST EXTRACT, SPICES, LEMON JUICE CONCENTRATE, CITRIC ACID.

Sample label for
Macaroni & Cheese

Nutrition Facts

(1) **Start Here** ➡

Serving Size 1 cup (228g)
Servings Per Container 2

(2) **Check Calories**

Amount Per Serving

Calories 250   Calories from Fat 110

	% Daily Value*	(6)
Total Fat 12g	18%	
Saturated Fat 3g	15%	
Trans Fat 3g		
Cholesterol 30mg	10%	
Sodium 470mg	20%	
Total Carbohydrate 31g	10%	
Dietary Fiber 0g	0%	
Sugars 5g		
Protein 5g		
Vitamin A	4%	
Vitamin C	2%	
Calcium	20%	
Iron	4%	

(3) **Limit these Nutrients**

(4) **Get Enough of these Nutrients**

Quick Guide to % DV

• **5% or less is Low**

• **20% or more is High**

* Percent Daily Values are based on a 2,000 calorie diet.
Your Daily Values may be higher or lower depending on
your calorie needs.

	Calories:	2,000	2,500
Total Fat	Less than	65g	80g
Sat Fat	Less than	20g	25g
Cholesterol	Less than	300mg	300mg
Sodium	Less than	2,400mg	2,400mg
Total Carbohydrate		300g	375g
Dietary Fiber		25g	30g

(5) **Footnote**

Exercise Goal-Setting Worksheet

NAME _____ GOAL START DATE _____

My Exercise Goal is: _____

_____

_____

_____

Goal Completion Date: _____

I will know I have reached my goal because: _____

_____

_____

_____

Three things that will help me reach my goal:

1 _____

2 _____

3 _____

Two people who can help me reach my goal:

1 _____

2 _____

Steps to reaching my goal: _____

_____

_____

_____

_____

_____

Relaxation Goal-Setting Worksheet

NAME _____ GOAL START DATE _____

My Relaxation Goal is: _____

_____

_____

_____

Goal Completion Date: _____

I will know I have reached my goal because: _____

_____

_____

_____

Three things that will help me reach my goal:

1 _____

2 _____

3 _____

Two people who can help me reach my goal:

1 _____

2 _____

Steps to reaching my goal: _____

_____

_____

_____

_____

_____

Recreation Goal-Setting Worksheet

NAME _____ GOAL START DATE _____

My Recreation Goal is: _____

_____

_____

_____

Goal Completion Date: _____

I will know I have reached my goal because: _____

_____

_____

_____

Three things that will help me reach my goal:

1 _____

2 _____

3 _____

Two people who can help me reach my goal:

1 _____

2 _____

Steps to reaching my goal: _____

_____

_____

_____

_____

_____

Relationships Goal-Setting Worksheet

NAME _____ GOAL START DATE _____

My Relationships Goal is: _____

_____

_____

_____

Goal Completion Date: _____

I will know I have reached my goal because: _____

_____

_____

_____

Three things that will help me reach my goal:

1 _____

2 _____

3 _____

Two people who can help me reach my goal:

1 _____

2 _____

Steps to reaching my goal: _____

_____

_____

_____

_____

_____

Nature Goal-Setting Worksheet

NAME _____ GOAL START DATE _____

My Nature Goal is: _____

_____

_____

_____

Goal Completion Date: _____

I will know I have reached my goal because: _____

_____

_____

_____

Three things that will help me reach my goal:

1 _____

2 _____

3 _____

Two people who can help me reach my goal:

1 _____

2 _____

Steps to reaching my goal: _____

_____

_____

_____

_____

_____

Giving Back Worksheet

NAME _____ MONTH/YEAR _____

Date/Time	Helping Act	For Whom	Where	How I Felt

Monthly Community Service Commitments

NAME_____ DATE_____

Ways I Currently Help Others	Frequency (Daily, Monthly; Hours)

I am currently not helping others because _____

_____

_____

_____

_____

_____

Spirituality Goal-Setting Worksheet

NAME _____ GOAL START DATE _____

My Spirituality Goal is: _____

_____

_____

_____

Goal Completion Date: _____

I will know I have reached my goal because: _____

_____

_____

_____

Three things that will help me reach my goal:

1 _____

2 _____

3 _____

Two people who can help me reach my goal:

1 _____

2 _____

Steps to reaching my goal: _____

_____

_____

_____

_____

_____

Values Worksheet

To foster spirituality in your lifestyle, examine your own values. Ask yourself:

1. What defines me as a person?

2. What role has religion or spirituality played in my life?

3. What is important to me?

4. How well do my daily activities reflect my values?

5. Do I neglect issues that matter to me because I'm busy spending time on things that matter less?

6. What are my important relationships?

7. What people give me a sense of community?

8. What/who inspires me and gives me hope?

9. What brings me joy?

10. What are my proudest achievements?

Leader's Guide

You may be a mental health professional leading a group of teens in inpatient or outpatient treatment. Or, you may be working mostly with teens you are seeing in treatment. Either way, this workbook can be used effectively to guide patients to optimize their mental health.

Always begin at the beginning! Have your patient/client start this process by reading and responding in writing to the Introductory Chapter. This sets the tone and the stage to advance through the subsequent chapters in any order that is desired. If this is a group enterprise, after the introductory material has been completed and each member has presented their intentions to you or to the group, the *8 Ways* chapters can be done sequentially or in any order chosen by you or group members.

If this is an inpatient or an outpatient group, whereby patients admit in an ongoing basis, have the newly admitted patient read over and complete the introductory material and then join the group in whatever chapter they happen to be working on. The point is that there is no particular order needed or required to addressing the chapters and their activities.

This workbook can be completed as quickly or in as leisurely a manner as your time and schedule permits. However, the main thing is to remind teens that this workbook can be with them for a lifetime, as there are always improvements to be made and areas needing attention to achieve a more balanced lifestyle. The idea is to have good information about optimizing mental health, resilience and wellbeing, and a means of keeping track of progress, continuing to make adjustments to Therapeutic Lifestyle Changes as needed.

Feel free to add other materials, amplify what has been provided, and in any other way teach and ground the material offered here.

Here's to a vibrant and healthy life!

CERTIFICATE OF ACHIEVEMENT

This Acknowledges That

_____

Has Successfully Explored and Implemented

8 Ways To Sustainable Wellbeing: For Teens and Their Families

This _____ Day of _____ 20 ____

Manufactured by Amazon.ca
Bolton, ON

38213586R00107